Beyond Boundaries

Insights into Culture and Communication

Cecilia Ikeguchi   Kyoko Yashiro

KINSEIDO

Kinseido Publishing Co., Ltd.
3-21 Kanda Jimbo-cho, Chiyoda-ku,
Tokyo 101-0051, Japan

Copyright © 2008 by Cecilia Ikeguchi
      Kyoko Yashiro

All rights reserved. No part of this publication may be reproduced, stored in a retrieval system, or transmitted, in any form or by any means, electronic, mechanical, photocopying, recording or otherwise, without the prior permission of the publisher.

Design: Hull corporation
Illustrations: illustrators moco

はしがき

　本書は、英語で異文化コミュニケーションを学ぶことにより、英語の読解能力を養い、同時に異文化コミュニケーションの基礎知識を習得することを目的として作成した。さらに異文化理解への積極的な態度とスキルを育成することを重要な目的と考え、体験学習的な活動を導入した。

　本書の特徴は、①異文化コミュニケーションの理論を日常的な例を多く示しながら平易に解説している reading text、②読解力を養うための5種類の練習問題、③学習者の考え、感情に直接働きかける異文化コミュニケーション活動である。

　本書は3部から成っている。1部4課は非言語コミュニケーション、2部6課は言語コミュニケーション、3部5課は価値観と態度の多様性をそれぞれ扱っている。1課から順に学んでいくことを想定しているが、必ずしも順を追っていく必要はなく、学習者のニーズや興味に応じて、適切な課から学んでいってよい。

　各課は以下のように構成されている。

Warm-up
　写真やイラスト、簡単なクイズを用いて課のテーマに関心を喚起する。
Key words
　読解の手助けとなる語句を取り上げ、意味を確認するマッチングを行う。
Reading
　実例を多数示しながら異文化コミュニケーションの理論を500語前後で平易に解説する。
Exercises
　A　New words
　　　Key Words で取り上げた語句を習得できたか確認する問題。
　B　Read for the main ideas
　　　本文の要旨を把握しているか確認する練習問題。
　C　Read for details
　　　本文中の細かいが重要なポイントを把握しているか確認する問題。
　D　Read between the lines
　　　本文に出てきた文を2つ示し、どのような接続方法が最も適切であるかを判断する問題。
　E　Cloze listening
　　　本文の要旨を cloze test を用いて確認する問題。穴埋めをした後でCDを聞き答えをチェック。
ICC Activity
　異文化コミュニケーションで重要な自己気づき、他者気づき、異文化理解の態度を形成するためのワークシート、ケース・スタディ、グループ・ワークなどを用いた体験学習。

　本書を学習することで、国際化した社会で私たちが日常的に遭遇する異文化コミュニケーションを建設的で有意義な体験とすることができるようになることを期待している。

2007年10月

池口セシリア　　八代京子

Table of Contents

Unit I: Non-verbal Communication

- Chapter 1: Facial Communication and Eye Contact 1
  表情とアイコンタクト
- Chapter 2: Gestures and Body Movement 9
  身振りと手振り
- Chapter 3: Space and Distance 16
  対人距離
- Chapter 4: Time in Communication 23
  時間の概念

Unit II Communicating with Words

- Chapter 5: Gender and Communication Style 31
  男女のコミュニケーション・スタイル
- Chapter 6: Culture and Communication Style 39
  文化とコミュニケーション・スタイル
- Chapter 7: Self-disclosure 47
  自己開示
- Chapter 8: Self-assertiveness 54
  自分の意見や考えを主張する
- Chapter 9: Active Listening 61
  アクティブ・リスニング
- Chapter 10: Conflict Management 68
  問題の解決

Unit III: Diversity in Values

- Chapter 11: Cultural Values 76
  価値観の違い
- Chapter 12: Ethnocentrism 83
  自文化中心主義
- Chapter 13: Barriers to Communication: Stereotypes 91
  コミュニケーションの障壁：ステレオタイプ
- Chapter 14: Barriers to Communication: Prejudice 98
  コミュニケーションの障壁：偏見
- Chapter 15: Barriers to Communication: Discrimination 105
  コミュニケーションの障壁：差別

References 112

Chapter 1 Facial Communication and Eye Contact

"In international relationships, our face communicates our emotions."
「国際コミュニケーションでは，表情が感情を伝える」(Ekman, 1987)

Warm-up

Look at the following pictures and answer the question below.

| 1 | 2 | 3 | 4 |

_____   _____   _____   _____

Q How does each person above feel? Choose one word below that describes the person's feelings above.

[angry / happy / sad / scared]

Key words

Match the words in the left column with their meaning in the right column. This will help you understand the reading passage.

1. cultural universal (   )   a．アイコンタクト、視線
2. express dissatisfaction (   )   b．怪しげな男
3. a stern face (   )   c．厳しい表情
4. get embarrassed (   )   d．視線の強さ／弱さ
5. eye contact (   )   e．視線の頻度の多さ／少なさ
6. mutual gaze (   )   f．知らない人をじっと見つめる
7. a high/low frequency of eye gaze (   )   g．恥ずかしい気持ちになる
8. a high/low intensity of eye gaze (   )   h．不満な気持ちを表す
9. a suspicious man (   )   i．文化的普遍性
10. stare at strangers (   )   j．凝視（すること）

1

READING

Facial expressions are the most important type of nonverbal communication. Our face communicates eight different kinds of emotions: anger, fear, disgust, surprise, sadness, happiness, interest and disappointment. Paul Ekman, a famous researcher, labels these emotions cultural universals. People from various cultural backgrounds recognize the same emotions in these facial expressions.

In the West, most individuals smile to show happiness or to express interest in something. A smile is also the most common form of greeting. However, a smile can convey a different emotion in some cultures. In Thailand, a smile can mean many things. People smile when they are angry, when they are physically hurt, or when they express dissatisfaction. In Japan people do not show too much emotion through facial expressions. A stern and serious face is a sign of sincerity and refined personal character. A smile can show a wide range of meanings. In the past, a bride was not allowed to smile during her wedding ceremony. In daily life, some people smile when they get embarrassed, or refrain from showing any emotion at all on their face. Smiling and laughing are ways to hide displeasure, sorrow and embarrassment, especially when one makes a mistake. Compared to Westerners, Japanese had been perceived as lacking in facial expressions, but this is gradually changing now.

Our eyes are regarded as the most important part of the face and they communicate many things. In daily conversations, eye contact is important, especially in intercultural communication, because very little or too much eye contact can cause communication problems. Eye communication shows many things, such as a person's attentiveness or the closeness of a relationship. For example, a researcher named Michael Argyle says that when eye contact goes beyond 60%, the people talking are very interested in each other. There are no strict rules about how much eye contact is necessary, but the degree of eye contact people need and use differs from culture to culture.

Research around the world on eye contact, also called mutual gaze, shows that most Americans and Arabs have a high frequency of mutual gaze. In face-to-face communication, most Americans consider someone who cannot maintain good eye contact as dishonest, suspicious, or inattentive. It shows a lack of interest in the other person. Compared to Americans, however, Arabs look at each other's eyes with such a high degree of intensity that it would make most Americans feel uncomfortable. Although eye contact is important in the U.S., in certain parts of the country, it is considered rude to stare at strangers. In the U.K. eye gaze shows attentive listening.

Some cultures, however, perceive eye contact differently. The Japanese, for example, show very low gaze frequency. Too much eye contact may be considered impolite and disrespectful, especially to someone higher in rank or status. In the classroom, a student lowers his eyes as a sign of respect for the teacher. That is why Western teachers are surprised when Japanese students look down while talking to them. In the same manner, an office clerk will keep his or her eyes down while talking to the boss.

EXERCISES

A New words

Circle the letter that gives the correct meaning of the underlined words/phrases.

1. Cultural universals are
   a. emotions that are the same for people in most cultures.
   b. faces that are the same for people in most cultures.
   c. expressions that are the same for people in most cultures.

2. A person gets embarrassed when
   a. he/she greets someone from another culture.
   b. he/she feels sad or lonely.
   c. he/she makes a mistake in front of people.

3. Someone with a stern face usually has
   a. a funny face.
   b. a serious face.
   c. a smiling face.

4. The statement "Japanese had been perceived as lacking in facial expressions" means

    a. they showed emotions on their faces.
    b. they did not show emotions on their faces.
    c. they communicated through their faces.
5. In face to face communication, <u>mutual gaze</u> means
    a. the speakers look straight at each other's eyes.
    b. the speakers avoid each other's eyes.
    c. the speakers look in opposite directions.
6. The expression "<u>a smile can convey a different emotion</u>" means
    a. people's emotions change according to their faces.
    b. people's eye contact changes according to their faces.
    c. people smile for different reasons at different times

B Read for the main ideas

Choose the answer that best completes the meaning of the sentence.

1. Sentence number four in the first paragraph is trying to say that most people around the world
    a. cry when they are very sad and smile when they are happy.
    b. hide their emotions according to their culture.
    c. have similar methods of eye contact depending on their feelings.
2. In the West, most people smile to
    a. greet others and show feelings.
    b. greet others and show sincerity.
    c. greet others and show embarrassment.
3. In different Asian countries, people smile to
    a. show they are embarrassed.
    b. show they are physically hurt.
    c. show different kinds of feelings.
4. In Europe, someone who has good eye contact
    a. is considered a close friend of the other person.
    b. is considered an attentive listener.
    c. is considered uninterested and dishonest.

5. In North America, a person with little eye contact
    a. is considered a close friend of the other persons.
    b. is considered uninterested or dishonest.
    c. is considered an attentive listener.
6. The fourth paragraph suggests that most people in Arab countries
    a. have more intense eye contact compared with North Americans.
    b. have less intense eye contact compared with North Americans.
    c. have the same degree of eye contact compared with North Americans.

C Read for details

Choose the answer that best completes the meaning of the sentence.

1. The passage suggests that the human face communicates
    a. six different kinds of emotions.
    b. eight different kinds of emotions.
    c. ten different kinds of emotions.
2. Which of the following is true of Thai people?
    a. They smile to hide their feelings.
    b. They smile to show they are happy.
    c. They smile to show different kinds of feelings.
3. According to the passage, a serious face in the Japanese culture shows
    a. a loving friendly person.
    b. an intelligent and serious person.
    c. a sincere and trustworthy character.
4. Thai and Japanese people are similar because
    a. they smile to hide their feelings.
    b. they smile to show they are happy.
    c. they smile to show different kinds of feelings.
5. Argyle says that when eye contact is beyond 60%
    a. the people talking are shy.
    b. the people talking like each other.

    c. the people talking like each other's face.
6. Western teachers are surprised when
    a. Japanese students look at their teachers when talking face to face.
    b. Japanese students look at each other's eyes during conversations.
    c. Japanese students look down while talking to the teacher.
7. How much eye contact is necessary?
    a. Very little eye contact creates intercultural communication problems.
    b. Too much eye contact creates intercultural communication problems.
    c. There are no strict rules about how much eye contact is necessary.

D Read between the lines

Choose the word/phrase that best connects the meanings of the sentence pair.

1. 1) Ekman, a famous researcher, calls these emotions cultural universals.
   2) People from various cultural backgrounds recognize the same emotions in facial expressions.
       a. this means   b. as a result   c. therefore

2. 1) A smile can show different emotions in some cultures.
   2) In Thailand, a smile has many different meanings.
       a. as a result   b. therefore   c. for example

3. 1) In Thailand, People sometimes smile when they are angry, physically hurt, or when they express dissatisfaction.
   2) In Japan, people do not show too much emotion through facial expressions.
       a. similarly   b. in contrast   c. certainly

4. 1) Studies on eye contact around the world show that most Americans and Arabs have a high frequency of mutual gaze.
   2) In face-to-face communication, most North Americans think someone who can not keep eye contact is dishonest, suspicious, or inattentive.
       a. certainly   b. in contrast   c. furthermore

5. 1) Too much eye contact may be considered impolite and disrespectful especially to someone higher in rank or status in Japan.

2) In the classroom, a student lowers his eyes as a sign of respect for the teacher.

   a. furthermore   b. in contrast   c. that is why

E Cloze listening

Fill in the gaps with words/phrases from below. Then, listen to the recording and check your answers.

> 1. can cause   2. terrible grief   3. express dissatisfaction
> 4. physically hurt   5. strict rules   6. different emotion
> 7. of greeting   8. tend to   9. serious face   10. get embarrassed

A person's face tells others so much about their feelings. We smile when we are happy; we cry when we are sad and in a_____.

In Japan, people do not show too much emotion through facial expressions. A stern or b_____ is a sign of sincerity and refined personal character. A smile in Japan can have different meanings compared to other societies. For example, people c_____ smile or laugh not only to show happiness but also to hide displeasure, sorrow or embarrassment. In daily life, some people smile when they d_____, or would not show any emotions at all in their faces. Smiling and laughing are ways to hide displeasure, sorrow and embarrassment especially when one makes a mistake.

In the West, most individuals smile to show happiness or when something is interesting. A smile is also the most common form e_____. However, a smile can convey a f_____ in some cultures. In Thailand, a smile can mean different things. People smile when they are angry, when they are g_____, or when they h_____.

Our eyes are regarded as the most important part of the face and they communicate many things. In daily conversations, eye contact is important, especially in intercultural communication because very little or too much eye contact i_____ communication problems. Eye contact shows many things

20 such as a person's attentiveness or closeness in a relationship. There are no j_____ about how much eye contact is necessary, but the degree of eye contact that people need differs from culture to culture.

ICC Activity

A Work with a partner. Choose one of the emotions below and make a facial expression to show that emotion. Your partner will guess the emotion in your face. Take turns.

1. happiness 2. interest 3. sadness 4. anger 5. fear

B Check your eye gaze. Tell the short story that your teacher will give you to a classmate.

<u>1st reading</u> Look at your classmate all the time while reading the story. How did you feel? Discuss.

<u>2nd reading</u> Read, but do not look at your classmate. Ask how your classmate felt. Discuss.

<u>3rd reading</u> Read, looking occasionally at your classmate's eyes. Did you feel any difference during these three times? Discuss.

Chapter 2 Gestures and Body Movement

"People in interactions move together in a kind of a dance, but they are unaware of this synchronous movement." (Hall, 1981)

「コミュニケーションをとっているとき、人は互いにダンスをしているように動くが、この動きを意識していない」

Warm-up

Match the following pictures and their meaning. Write the number of the picture on the lines provided.

1　　　　　　2　　　　　　3　　　　　　4

_____ OK.　　　　　　　　　_____ Come Here.

_____ I can't hear you.　　　　_____ No. Not good!

Key words

Match the words in the left column with their meaning in the right column. This will help you understand the reading passage.

1. a source of confusion （　　）　　a. 混乱の源
2. cultural variations （　　）　　　b. 洗練されたジェスチャー
3. obscene gestures （　　）　　　　c. 沈黙のことば
4. beckon *someone* （　　）　　　　d. 人のまねをする
5. refined gestures （　　）　　　　e. 人を招き寄せる
6. universal greeting （　　）　　　f. 卑猥なジェスチャー
7. imitate *someone* （　　）　　　　g. 普遍的な挨拶
8. silent language （　　）　　　　　h. 文化の多様性

READING

When we travel to another country, we soon find out that not all gestures and body movements are universal in meaning. Differences in gestures and body movements across cultures are often a source of confusion. This is because people express their emotions and feelings in different ways. People in many countries express friendship by kissing and hugging. In the U.S., for example, kissing is a very common physical expression of emotion, and it is also a form of greeting. Although kissing is found in all cultures, there are a lot of cultural variations. In Arab countries, it is common for men to kiss and hold each other's hands, but not in the U.S. In other societies, it is common for women to hold hands.

Gestures are certain movements of the body that carry meaning. People across the world talk with their hands, but what they say depends on their culture. Hand gestures carry different meanings that vary from culture to culture, and can be very confusing in face to face communication. The "OK" sign (formed by circling the index finger and the thumb) and the "Good Luck" sign (formed by closing the fist with the thumb pointed up) may have positive meanings in the U.S., but are considered obscene in some South American countries. In Japan, the "OK" gesture, with circled fingers facing to the outside, means "money." Another example is the gesture for "Come here," or the beckoning sign, which differs across cultures. To beckon someone with the palm up is common in the United States, but is considered rude in some Asian countries, where the gesture would indicate calling an animal. Still another example of cultural variation in gestures is the sign for "Me." In the U.S., "Me" or "I" is indicated by pointing to one's chest; in Japan, however, one would point to one's nose. Prof. Satoshi Ishii wrote that Japanese generally prefer refined, quiet types of gestures called "*shigusa*" rather than the free and overly expressive types of gestures called "*miburi*."

Another important body movement with many cultural variations is the handshake. The handshake is a universal type of greeting. There are different types of handshakes all across the world that vary depending on how long and how strong people shake hands. Strong or firm handshakes and weak or limp handshakes can be either short or long. A firm handshake is characterized by strong hand contact while the limp handshake is gentle and weak. Each of these types can last a few seconds to as long as the greeting lasts.

We learn the gestures of our culture unconsciously from childhood. We imitate the people we see around us without knowing what they mean. What may be considered common and polite in one culture may be regarded as strange and rude in another. To communicate with people from another culture, it is important to know the "silent" language of that culture.

EXERCISES

A New words

Circle the letter that gives the correct meaning of the underlined words/phrases.

1. Cultural variations in gestures means
   a. differences in the meaning of gestures from culture to culture.
   b. differences in the way people sign in many cultures.
   c. differences in the way people greet in many cultures.

2. "The 'Okay' sign in the U.S. has an obscene meaning in some other countries" indicates
   a. it has a positive meaning.
   b. it has a deep social meaning.
   c. it has a bad and offensive meaning.

3. In the passage, to beckon someone means
   a. to indicate someone.
   b. to call someone.
   c. to point to someone.

4. The handshake is a universal type of greeting. This means
   a. the handshake is used by people in some countries.
   b. the handshake is used by most people in most countries.
   c. the handshake is used by most people all across the world.

5. A firm handshake is tight and strong, while a limp handshake is

a. loose and gentle.
b. loose and long.
c. loose and short.

B Read for the main ideas

Choose the answer that best completes the meaning of the sentence.

1. According to the passage, gestures are
    a. body movements that have different meanings across cultures.
    b. body movements that have the same meanings across cultures.
    c. hand movements that express emotion across cultures.

2. In the U.S., people kiss when
    a. they are angry.
    b. they greet each other.
    c. they want to ask a favor.

3. In Arab countries, it is common for men to
    a. shake hands and kiss each other.
    b. hold hands and greet each other.
    c. hold hands and kiss each other.

4. Using our hands to communicate means,
    a. we use hand gestures.
    b. we use our face to communicate.
    c. we shake hands with the other person.

5. In the U.S., people indicate "I"
    a. by pointing to one's nose.
    b. by pointing to one's chest.
    c. by pointing to one's index finger.

6. In Japan, people indicate "I"
    a. by pointing to one's nose.
    b. by pointing to one's chest.
    c. by pointing to one's index finger.

Chapter 2 *Gestures and Body Movement*

C Read for details

Choose the answer that best completes the meaning of the sentence.

1. Differences in gestures and body movements across cultures
    a. cause problems in face-to-face communication.
    b. have positive meanings in most cultures.
    c. are physical expressions of emotion.

2. Which of the following is true of Asian gestures?
    a. Do not call someone with the palm up.
    b. Do not call someone with the palm down.
    c. Do not greet someone with a kiss.

3. Which of the following is true for Japanese people?
    a. They prefer quiet refined types of gestures.
    b. They prefer free and overly expressive gestures.
    c. They prefer both quiet and expressive gestures.

4. Which of the following statements is NOT true?
    a. The "shigusa" are the quiet, refined types of gestures.
    b. The "miburi" are free and expressive types of gestures.
    c. The "come here" sign in the U.S. means "money" in Japan.

5. The best way to communicate with people from a different culture is
    a. to know the silent messages of their language.
    b. to understand the silent language of their culture.
    c. to imitate what they do.

6. There are different types of handshakes depending on
    a. how long people shake hands.
    b. how strong people shake hands.
    c. how long and how strong people shake hands.

7. We learn the gestures of our culture by
    a. imitating people around us.
    b. listening to what people say.
    c. reading a lot of books.

D Read between the lines

Choose the word/phrase that best connects the meanings of the sentence pair.

1. 1) People express their emotions and feelings in different ways.
   2) People in some countries express friendship by kissing, but people in other countries don't.
      a. moreover   b. as a result   c. for example

2. 1) The "OK" sign and the "Good Luck" sign have positive meanings in the U.S.
   2) These are considered obscene in some South American countries.
      a. therefore   b. however   c. for example

3. 1) The handshake is a common type of greeting worldwide.
   2) There are different types of handshakes all across the world.
      a. furthermore   b. similarly   c. as a result

4. 1) A firm handshake is done with strong hand contact.
   2) A limp handshake is gentle and weak.
      a. similarly   b. therefore   c. in contrast

5. 1) What may be common and polite in one culture may be strange and rude in another.
   2) To communicate with people from another culture, it is important to know the "silent" language of that culture.
      a. therefore   b. on the contrary   c. finally

E Cloze listening

Fill in the gaps with words/phrases from below. Then, listen to the recording and check your answers.

1. most common   2. different types   3. and determined
4. same meanings   5. nonverbal messages 6. of confusion
7. hand gestures   8. have meaning   9. a weak   10. body movement

Chapter 2 Gestures and Body Movement

People all over the world communicate non-verbally using different signs or codes as well as body movements. Gestures are certain movements of the body that a_____. People express their emotions and feelings using gestures. Unfortunately, not all gestures and body movements have the b_____.
Differences in gestures and body movement across cultures are often a source c_____ in face-to-face communication.

Body movements carry a variety of d_____. These are expressed through facial expressions, eye movements, e_____, posture and movements of body parts such as arms, legs and feet. Hand gestures are the f_____ gestures people use all over the world to express non-verbal messages.

The handshake is an important g_____ that has many cultural variations. The handshake is a universal type of greeting. There are h_____ of handshakes all across the world depending on how long and how strong people shake hands. The strong handshake can mean a strong i_____ personality, while the soft handshake can mean j_____ and gentle personality. What is your handshake like?

ICC Activity

Work with a partner and do the following exercises.

1. Put your hands on your hips and look at your partner in the eye. Ask how he or she felt.
2. You tell a short story that your teacher will give you, with a serious face to a partner. The listener yawns while listening to the story. After telling the story, explain how you felt.
3. Pantomime the following thoughts. Your partner will guess what you mean.

   "I'm hungry."   "I don't know."   "This is a secret."
   "Go away."   "Be quiet."

Chapter 3 Space and Distance

"The way people use space communicates messages." (Klopf and Ishii, 1997)
「人と人の間の距離は大切なメッセージである」

Warm-up

Look at the following pictures and answer the questions below.

Q Picture 1   Guess who these people are. What is their relationship?

Picture 2   What is their relationship? What is the difference between picture 1 and picture 2?

Key words

Match the words in the left column with their meaning in the right column. This will help you understand the reading passage.

1. comfort zone (　　)   a. 後ずさりする
2. intimacy (　　)   b. 腕の長さの距離
3. intimate level (　　)   c. 快適な範囲
4. stand at a distance (　　) d. 攻撃的な
5. step back (　　)   e. 親密度
6. keep a distance (　　)   f. 親密さ
7. aggressive (　　)   g. 成立させる
8. an arm's length (　　)   h. 適切な距離を置く
9. establish (　　)   i. 離れて立つ

READING

When people talk face to face, there is a "bubble of space" between them, and the size of this bubble varies from culture to culture. This space has been given different names. Sometimes, it is called "conversational distance," sometimes "comfort zone," and sometimes "interpersonal distance." Generally, the space people keep between them when talking face to face can also tell us about their relationship and the situation. Space and intimacy go together. At the intimate level, people stand very close to each other, and speak with very low voices. At the social level, people stand not too far apart, and not too close, and use regular speaking voices. During small group discussions and meetings, the leader sits or stands where everyone in the group can see him or her. At the public level, as in making public speeches, the speaker stands at a distance and speaks with a louder voice than usual.

The distance people keep between themselves when talking varies across cultures. In some societies, this distance is big. This means that when a person comes too close, and the "bubble of space" is pressured the other person will feel uncomfortable. He will probably step back. In some societies, this distance is smaller. People feel comfortable standing closer to each other when talking face to face.

It is believed that people from cold climates keep greater distances from each other when talking than people from warm climates. For example, Latin Americans and people in Arab countries stand very close to each other during conversations. This is a sign of friendliness and familiarity. Most people in the West stand farther away from a person when talking face to face. If someone tries to come too close, they will move back. For them, standing too close is rude and feels aggressive. For example, for North Americans a comfortable distance is about an arm's length or up to about four feet. Standing closer than this is a sign of intimacy, meaning the people are emotionally close to each other. Compared to Americans, however, Japanese sometimes stand farther away from one another especially in business and formal situations. They need more space for bowing too.

Imagine when two people from different "space" cultures talk. A person from a small "space" culture will think the other person standing at a distance is "cold" and unfriendly. He might continue to move closer in an attempt to establish a friendly conversation. The other person, however, will think he is aggressive and rude by standing too close. He might continue to move back every time the other person comes closer. He will end up pushed up against a wall. Of course cultural differences do not explain everything about the way individuals behave.

Differences in the size of the "space bubble" is one cause of intercultural problems in non-verbal communication. It is wise to observe the bubble of space of the person you are talking to, especially if he or she is from a different culture.

EXERCISES

A New words

Circle the letter that gives the correct meaning of the underlined words/phrases.

1. Interpersonal distance is the study of space
    a. between people.
    b. between cultures.
    c. between groups.

2. When people talk at an intimate level, they speak with low voices and stand from the other person
    a. very close to each other
    b. far apart from each other
    c. comfortably away from each other

3. In the passage, to stand at a distance means to
    a. be intimate with someone.
    b. keep enough space when talking.
    c. speak with a loud voice.

4. To keep a distance means to stand
    a. very close to someone.
    b. side by side with someone.
    c. neither too close nor too far from someone.

5. In conversations, people keep an arm's length when they _____ from the other person.

18

a. stand closer than four feet away
b. stand farther than four feet away
c. stand about four feet away

B Read for the main ideas

Choose the answer that best completes the meaning of the sentence.

1. According to the passage, the "bubble of space"
   a. between people differs from culture to culture.
   b. between people is the same for all cultures.
   c. between people is very uncomfortable.

2. When someone comes very close to them, people from a "large bubble" society
   a. feel comfortable and think the other person is warm and friendly.
   b. feel uncomfortable and think the other person is rude and aggressive.
   c. feel disturbed and think the other person is emotionally too close.

3. Studies show that during conversations, people from cold climates generally
   a. stand farther apart when they talk.
   b. stand close to each other when they talk.
   c. feel uncomfortable when the other person is talking.

4. When someone tries to come too close, people from North America will
   a. try to move closer because they feel uncomfortable.
   b. try not to move because they will offend the other person.
   c. try to move back because they feel uncomfortable.

5. Japanese people stand farther away during conversations because
   a. they need space to shake hands.
   b. they need space to bow.
   c. they need space to be polite.

C Read for details

Choose the answer that best completes the meaning of the sentence.

1. At the intimate level, people stand very close to each other and speak
    a. with very low voices.
    b. with regular speaking voices.
    c. with voices louder than usual.

2. At the social level, people stand not too far apart from each other and speak
    a. with very low voices.
    b. with regular speaking voices.
    c. with voices louder than usual.

3. At the public level, the speaker stands at a distance and speaks
    a. with a very low voice.
    b. with a regular speaking voice.
    c. with a voice louder than usual.

4. In daily conversations, people from South America and Arab countries
    a. stand very close to each other.
    b. keep distance between themselves.
    c. talk with louder voices than usual.

5. If you stand far in conversations, most people from Arab countries will think
    a. you are respectful and kind.
    b. you are honest and polite.
    c. you are cold and unfriendly.

6. When you talk with someone from a different culture, you must
    a. check your speaking voice.
    b. check your bubble of space.
    c. check your speaking rate.

D Read between the lines

Choose the word/phrase that best connects the meanings of the sentence pair.

1. 1) Generally, the space people keep when talking face to face can tell us about their relationship.

Chapter 3 Space and Distance

    2) Space and intimacy go together.
        a. in other words   b. however   c. probably

2. 1) At the social level, people stand not too far and not too close, using regular speaking voices.
    2) During small group discussions and meetings, the leader sits or stands where everyone in the group can see him or her.
        a. probably   b. for example   c. on the contrary

3. 1) Latin Americans and people in Arab countries stand very close during conversations.
    2) Most people in the West stand farther apart when talking face to face.
        a. for example   b. finally   c. on the other hand

4. 1) Most people in the West stand fairly far apart when talking face to face.
    2) If someone tries to come too close, they will move back.
        a. on the other hand   b. for example   c. therefore

5. 1) Differences in the size of the "space bubble" is one cause of misunderstandings in face to face communication.
    2) It is wise to check your own bubble of space.
        a. however   b. so   c. as a result

E Cloze listening

Fill in the gaps with words/phrases from below. Then, listen to the recording and check your answers.

    1. move back   2. go together   3. their relationship   4. stand apart
    5. regular speaking   6. friendly conversation   7. interpersonal distance
    8. across cultures   9. very close   10. a distance

    Space is very important in human interaction and communication. The study of space in intercultural communication is called a_____. It explains how people unconsciously b_____ from each other during conversations.

The amount of space people use when communicating tells a great deal about c_____. At the intimate level, people stand d_____ to each other and speak with very low voices. At the social level, people stand not too far apart and not too close, and use e_____ voices. At the public level, such as when making public speeches, people stand at f_____ and speak with louder voices than usual. As you can see, space and intimacy g_____.

The distance people keep between themselves when talking varies h_____. In some societies, this distance is big. People stand far apart during conversations. In some societies, this distance is small. People stand close to each other during conversations.

Imagine when two people from different "space" cultures talk. A person from a "small space" culture will move closer to establish a i_____. A person from a "large space" culture will feel uncomfortable and try to j_____. One person will keep moving closer each time the other moves back. The other person will end up pushed against the wall.

ICC Activity

Check your bubble of space.

1. Choose a partner. One of you will stand at a regular distance, and talk about the weather. Next, you will move closer, and talk about the same topic. The third time, you will stand very close to the other person, close enough to hear him breathing. Which is the most comfortable conversation distance for you? That is your own "bubble space."

2. Take turns doing this. What is your partner's comfortable personal space?

Chapter 4 Time in Communication

"Time talks." (Hall, 1976)

「時間は語る」

Warm-up

Choose the answer that applies to you.

situation 1   You have an appointment at 12 noon with a friend for lunch. You will come:
  a. five minutes (or more) before 12 o'clock.
  b. five minutes (or more) after 12 o'clock.
  c. at exactly 12 o'clock.

situation 2   You are going out for a picnic with your classmates at 9 tomorrow. Assembly time is 8:30. What time will you come?
  a. 10–20 minutes before 8:30
  b. 10–20 minutes after 8:30
  c. between 8:25 and 8:30

situation 3   You have a job interview at 10 a.m. tomorrow. What time will you arrive?
  a. 30 min.–1 hour before 10 a.m.
  b. a few minutes [seconds] before 10 a.m.
  c. 10–15 minutes before 10 a.m.

Key words

Match the words in the left column with their meaning in the right column. This will help you understand the reading passage.

1. meet the deadline (　　)
2. keep an appointment (　　)
3. in a hurry (　　)
4. punctuality (　　)
5. monochronic time (　　)
6. polychronic time (　　)
7. specify (　　)
8. emergency (　　)

a. 急いで
b. M時間、時計時間
c. 緊急事態
d. 時間を守ること
e. 締め切りの時間を守る
f. P時間、課題時間
g. 明示する
h. 約束の時間を守る

READING

Our idea about time affects our communication patterns and our relationships with people. The agreed-upon time for many situations, like a date, a business meeting, or a party, has quite different meanings to different people. Promises to meet deadlines or keep appointments vary widely from culture to culture.

In some countries like North America, people create lists of activities one at a time. Therefore it is necessary to finish one thing in time to be able to do the next activity. An American will arrive on time for work, meetings, and parties and plans his schedule one week or one month ahead. He worries about having to wait for someone for ten minutes. People are oftentimes in a hurry. Punctuality is very important. People need a watch to be on time. They have a monochronic approach to time.

Not all cultures share the American attitude towards time. In some parts of the world like Latin America and Asia, individuals are quite relaxed about time. In these countries, people make a schedule of several things they have to do at the same time. They have a polychronic approach to time. It is common to be late, and to leisurely finish work. People are more patient waiting for someone who is late for an appointment. Punctuality is not so important for certain people. Generally the Japanese are extremely prompt when meeting someone at an appointed time. It is considered rude to keep someone waiting.

The arrival and departure times for social activities is also different across cultures. If an American invites you for dinner, he specifies what time the guest is expected to come. If he says "Come anytime," then probably the invitation is not sincere. In Greece, when someone says "Come to my house anytime" people really mean the guest is welcome anytime.

In Japan, social gatherings, especially parties, are carefully scheduled for a specific starting and ending time, after which people have to pack up and say goodbye. For example, parties and formal meetings that take place in public restaurants usually have a time limit of two hours. The times people choose to communicate also differ from country to country. Business calls usually take place from nine to five in most Western countries. For personal and social calls, it is considered rude to call someone by phone after nine in the evening. In New Zealand, it is considered impolite to make a phone call to someone after eight in the evening. A telephone call made at this time of day usually means that there is an emergency.

We usually learn the importance of time in communication early in life. No one teaches us; experience teaches us the best time for communicating. How we use time in different situations tells much about who we are to other people. It is very crucial in our personal relationships. So if a foreign friend comes 30 minutes late, do not be surprised.

EXERCISES

A New words

Circle the letter that gives the correct meaning of the underlined words/phrases.

1. <u>Agreed-upon situations</u> in the first paragraph refers to
    a. arriving on time for work
    b. fixing work schedules one week in advance.
    c. business meetings, parties, appointments or dates.

2. For a North American, <u>punctuality</u> means
    a. to be on time for every scheduled activity.
    b. to be on time for a meeting.
    c. to be on time for work.

3. People who have a <u>monochronic</u> approach to time
    a. are quite relaxed about time.
    b. have a list of things to do one at a time.
    c. have different things to do at the same time.

4. People who have a <u>polychronic</u> approach to time
    a. never come late for an appointment.
    b. have a list of things to do one at a time.
    c. have different things to do at the same time.

5. According to the third paragraph, to <u>be prompt</u> means

a. to make someone wait for an appointment.
b. to be on time for an appointment.
c. to keep a record of time.

6. Thinking about time is <u>crucial in our personal relationships</u> means
   a. it happens all the time when meeting people.
   b. it is very important when meeting people.
   c. it is a difficult problem in our daily life.

B Read for the main ideas

Choose the answer that best completes the meaning of the sentence.

1. Which of the following statements is NOT true?
   a. People's attitude towards time varies from culture to culture.
   b. Greeks have a monochronic approach to time.
   c. Japanese are generally strict about time.

2. Americans' attitude towards time is called
   a. monochronic.
   b. polychronic.
   c. monotonic.

3. "People who have a polychronic approach to time …" means
   a. they are more relaxed about punctuality rules.
   b. they are stricter about punctuality rules.
   c. they speak up and say goodbye.

4. In countries where people have polychronic time,
   a. they do one thing at a time.
   b. they do several things at the same time.
   c. they do their work after their appointments.

5. In most countries, late evening phone calls are considered
   a. emergencies.
   b. rude and friendly.
   c. polite and friendly.

6. The third paragraph is trying to say that

a. Japanese are not patient when waiting for people who are late.

b. Japanese are polite when waiting for people who are late.

c. Japanese think it is rude to be late for an appointment.

C Read for details

Choose the answer that best completes the meaning of the sentence.

1. It is important for people in North America to finish one thing at a time because
   a. they need to do the next activity.
   b. they are always in a rush.
   c. they need a watch all the time.

2. In some countries in Latin America, people are
   a. very unhappy being late for an appointment.
   b. more relaxed in inviting people to their homes.
   c. more patient when waiting for people who are late.

3. Usually when an American invites someone for dinner,
   a. he is serious about the invitation.
   b. he is not serious about the invitation.
   c. he mentions the exact time for dinner.

4. In some Asian countries, when someone says "Come to my home,"
   a. the guest is welcome some time later.
   b. the guest is welcome at the specified time.
   c. the guest is welcome anytime.

5. Social gatherings, like parties, in Japan usually
   a. take place in the afternoon.
   b. take place within a fixed length of time.
   c. take place on weekends.

6. According to the passage, we usually start to learn the importance of time
   a. when we are small.
   b. when we go to school.
   c. when we travel to other places.

D Read between the lines

Choose the word/phrase that best connects the meanings of the sentence pair.

1. 1) The agreed-upon time for many situations, like a date or a meeting, or a party, has different meanings to different people.
   2) Promises to keep appointments vary widely from culture to culture.
       a. this means   b. therefore   c. in contrast

2. 1) Punctuality is very important.
   2) People need a watch to be on time.
       a. however   b. therefore   c. in contrast

3. 1) People have a polychronic approach to time.
   2) People make a schedule of several things they have to do at the same time.
       a. probably   b. as a result   c. this means

4. 1) If an American invites you for dinner, and says "Come anytime," the invitation is probably not sincere.
   2) In Greece when someone says "Come anytime to my house" he really means the guest is welcome any time.
       a. similarly   b. therefore   c. in contrast

5. 1) In Japan, social gatherings usually take place during a fixed period of time.
   2) Parties and formal meetings in public places usually have a two hour limit.
       a. however   b. for example   c. as a result

E Cloze listening

Fill in the gaps with words/phrases from below. Then, listen to the recording and check your answers.

1. time period   2. in a rush   3. attitudes and values
4. about punctuality   5. early in life   6. leisurely finish
7. extremely prompt   8. less important

Chapter 4 Time in Communication

When there is a gathering of international friends, and the meeting time is at 9 o'clock, some people will come at 8:30; some will come at 8:55 or exactly 9 o'clock, and others will come at 9:30 or even later. Why is this so? The reason lies in the different a_____ people have about time.

In some regions like North America, punctuality is very important. People usually have a list of activities to do one at a time. It is important to finish one thing on time to be able to do the next activity. An American goes to work on time, starts and finishes a meeting on time; goes to meet a friend, and worries if a friend is late by ten minutes. People always seem to be b_____. People have a monochronic sense of time. Other cultures, however, are different. For example, in some regions like Latin America and the Middle East, individuals are quite unconcerned c_____. People make a schedule of several things they have to do at the same time. They have a polychronic sense of time. It is common to be late and d_____ work. People are more patient when waiting for someone who is late for an appointment. Punctuality in these countries is e_____.

The Japanese, like most Americans, are f_____ in keeping time, and meeting someone for an appointment. It is considered rude to keep someone waiting. Even social gatherings, such as parties, usually take place within a g_____ of two hours. Formal activities, like wedding parties, sometimes last a little longer.

We usually learn the importance of time h_____. No one teaches us; experience teaches us the best time for communication. It is very crucial in our personal relationships. So if a foreign friend comes 30 minutes late, do not be surprised.

29

ICC Activity

1. Check your knowledge of world approach to time. Write T or F.

   1) If you work in Africa, you should rush when doing business. _____
   2) In Brazil, you must come at 8:55 if you have an appointment at 9:00. _____
   3) It is common to be late for evening parties in Canada. _____
   4) In Argentina, showing up 30 minutes late for a party is rude. _____
   5) You must be on time if you have a business meeting in Italy. _____

2. Check your answers with your teacher. The information here will tell you that people's attitudes toward time are very different across cultures.

Chapter 5 Gender and Communication Style

"Men and women live in different worlds...made of different words." (Tannen, 2001)

「話し方を見ていると、男と女はあたかも別の世界に住んでいるように思える」

Warm-up

Answer the following questions.

1. Think of your family. If you are a female student, do you like to go shopping with your brother/father? If you are a male student, do you like to go shopping? Alone or with someone?

2. Why?

Key words

Match the words in the left column with their meaning in the right column. This will help you understand the reading passage.

1. gender differences (　　)
2. interaction (　　)
3. overgeneralization (　　)
4. build connections (　　)
5. compete (　　)
6. wedding anniversary (　　)
7. give an order (= order) (　　)
8. judge men by women's standard (　　)

a. 一般化しすぎること
b. 女の人の基準で男の人を判断する
c. 競争する、競合する
d. 結婚記念日
e. コネをつくる、関係を築く
f. 性差
g. 命令する
h. やり取り

READING

Many people have studied the ways men and women speak. They have found out that there are gender differences in ways of speaking. Men and women, and boys and girls, speak differently in face-to-face conversations. We need to identify and understand these differences to be able to build better relationships.

Have you ever heard someone say: "Men are interested in information; women are interested in interaction"? Some people say this is an overgeneralization. Deborah Tannen, a well-known writer, says this does not mean that women are not interested in information. The truth is, both men and women are interested in information. When girls talk, they usually engage in rapport-talk while boys do the report-talk. Rapport-talk is about personal information, while report-talk is about impersonal information. When girls sit down and talk, they share secrets and exchange personal information. They talk about personal problems—their own or other people's problems. Girls like sharing information to establish relationships, deepen friendships and maintain connections. When boys sit side by side, they usually talk about sports, cars, computers, or hobbies. These topics are considered impersonal information. Boys enjoy exchanging impersonal information as a way to show their expertise or skills. This is called impersonal talk. They establish friendships and build connections in a different way than girls. Boys connect to each other through friendly competition, while girls compete to establish a connection.

Another interesting difference is that girls usually remember smaller details and tend to talk a lot about them. Boys think girls are wasting time when they do this. On the other hand, girls think men are very cold and unfriendly. This is why women get upset when men forget their birthday or wedding anniversary. A famous story goes like this: the day before Mary's birthday, her boyfriend Tony asked her what she would like for a present. Mary said smiling, "Don't worry about it." The next day, Mary was upset when her boyfriend came back without a gift. Tony asked, "What's wrong?" Mary answered, "Why didn't you buy me a present?" Tony replied: "I asked you but you said you didn't need one." Mary responded "Did you really think I meant it?"

Still another basic difference, which is very similar to the idea above, is that women tend to be more indirect than men. This is especially true in the workplace and in personal relationships. Women managers do not give direct orders because they think people will do their work without being given orders. Unfortunately, sometimes men do not understand the meanings of these indirect requests.

Some experts say men should try to talk more like women. When experts say this, they are judging men by women's standards. On the other hand, some experts say women should talk more like men. When they say this, they are judging women by men's standards. Moreover, culture influences gender communication. Understanding differences in conversation style is a big step towards communication and building relationships.

EXERCISES

A New words

Circle the letter that gives the correct meaning of the underlined words/phrases.

1. There are gender differences in ways of speaking means
    a. men and women speak differently.
    b. men ask more questions than women.
    c. men and women talk about their personal problems.

2. "Women are not interested in information" is an overgeneralization. This means
    a. all women are not in interested in information.
    b. some women are interested in information.
    c. both men and women are not interested in information.

3. According to the passage, impersonal talk includes
    a. topics about one's friends and teachers.
    b. topics about cars and computers.
    c. topics about problems in the family.

4. When men and women talk, they connect to each other. This means that they
    a. forget about their friendship.

b. talk about their friendship.

c. keep their friendship going.

5. According to the passage, when experts judge women by men's standards
   a. they want men to behave and talk like women.
   b. they want women to behave and talk like men.
   c. they want men and women to change their speaking style.

B Read for the main ideas

Choose the answer that best completes the meaning of the sentence.

1. It is important to understand gender differences in communication
   a. to enjoy traveling overseas.
   b. to build better relationships.
   c. to study how men and women talk.

2. Deborah Tannen says that in daily conversations
   a. men are interested in information.
   b. women are interested in interaction.
   c. men and women are interested in information.

3. According to the passage, when girls exchange personal information
   a. they do the rapport-talk.
   b. they do the report-talk.
   c. they do the interactive talk.

4. According to the passage, when boys talk and exchange information
   a. they do the rapport-talk.
   b. they do the report-talk.
   c. they do the interactive talk.

5. In the workplace, women managers do not give direct orders because
   a. staff are intelligent enough to understand orders.
   b. staff are stupid and will not understand orders anyway.
   c. staff understand what they are supposed to do without orders.

Chapter 5 *Gender and Communication Style*

C Read for details

Choose the answer that best completes the meaning of the sentence.

1. When girls talk a lot about small things, boys think that
    a. girls are wasting their time.
    b. girls are cold and unfriendly.
    c. girls remember a lot of details.

2. Girls like to talk and share information in order to
    a. show their skills.
    b. establish relationships and deepen friendships.
    c. show that they remember small things.

3. Husbands usually forget wives' birthdays because
    a. men are usually careless.
    b. men do not usually love their wives.
    c. men do not usually remember small things.

4. In the passage, Mary was upset because
    a. Tony forgot her birthday.
    b. Tony asked about her birthday.
    c. Tony did not buy her a birthday present.

5. Some experts suggest that
    a. men should try to talk more like women.
    b. women should try to talk less.
    c. gender communication is unnatural.

D Read between the lines

Choose the word/phrase that best connects the meanings of the sentence pair.

1. 1) Studies have found that there are gender differences in ways of speaking.
   2) Men and women, and boys and girls, speak differently in face-to-face conversations.
      a. in other words   b. however   c. consequently

35

2. 1) Girls are interested in people when they talk.
   2) This does not mean that girls are not interested in information.
      a. however   b. similarly   c. otherwise

3. 1) When girls sit face to face, they exchange information about themselves and other people.
   2) When boys sit side by side, they usually talk about cars, computers and exchange information to show their skills.
      a. at the same time   b. by the way   c. on the other hand

4. 1) Rapport-talk is about personal information while report-talk is about impersonal information.
   2) When girls sit and talk, they share secrets and exchange personal information.
      a. however   b. that means   c. similarly

5. 1) In the workplace, women tend to be more indirect than men.
   2) Women managers do not give direct orders.
      a. for example   b. however   c. on the contrary

E Cloze listening

Fill in the gaps with words/phrases from below. Then, listen to the recording and check your answers.

1. their expertise   2. and understand   3. impersonal information
4. remember small things   5. sharing information   6. wasting time
7. big step   8. more indirect   9. personal information
10. and unfriendly

There are gender differences in ways of speaking. Men and women speak differently in face-to-face conversations. We need to identify a_____ these differences to be able to build better relationships.

When girls talk, they usually do the rapport-talk while boys do the report-talk.

Chapter 5 Gender and Communication Style

5   When girls sit down and talk, they share secrets and exchange b_____.
They talk about personal problems – their own or other people's problems. Girls like
c_____ to establish relationships, deepen friendships and maintain
connections. When boys sit side by side, they usually talk about sports, cars,
computers, or hobbies. This is called d_____. Boys enjoy talking about
10 these topics as a way to show e_____ or skills. They establish friendships
and build connections in a different way. Boys connect to each other through
friendly competition, while girls compete to establish a connection.

   Another interesting difference is that girls usually f_____ better and
tend to talk a lot about them. Boys think girls are g_____ when they
15 do this. On the other hand, girls think men are very cold h_____.
Furthermore, some studies say that women tend to be i_____ than men,
especially at work and in personal relationships. Understanding differences in
conversation styles is a j_____ towards communication and building
relationships.

37

ICC Activity

A Check your gender consciousness. Write your answers and discuss with a partner.

1. Who do you think should do the following, Men or Women?
    1) Clean the house   2) Cook   3) Wash clothes/dishes
    4) Take care of children

2. Who do you think can do the following jobs better? Why? Discuss with a partner.
    1) Cooking   2) Cleaning the house   3) Taking care of children
    4) Teaching   5) Engineering   6) Taking orders in the military

B Guess where the following conversation takes place. Guess who is the man and who is the woman. Why do you think so?

   A: What do you think of this brown shirt?
   B: It's OK.
   A: What about this blue one?
   B: That's OK too.
   A: Which one do you think fits me better?
   B: Both of them look good on you.
   A: Which one do you think I should buy?
   B: You can buy either the blue or the brown. It doesn't matter to me.

Chapter 6 Culture and Communication Style

"The words people use and the way they are put together tell much about a particular culture." (Gundykunst and Ting-Toomey, 1998)

「人がどのようにことばを使って表現しているかを観察すると、その文化の特徴がよくわかる」

Warm-up

What would you say in the following situations?

1) Someone says "You're beautiful."
2) You disagree with what your teacher just said.
3) Your friend invited you out to dinner, but you don't feel like going.

"You're beautiful!"   "I don't think so…"   "I don't want to…"

Key words

Match the words in the left column with their meaning in the right column. This will help you understand the reading passage.

1. a nation of immigrants ( ) 　　a. 移民国家
2. a homogenous culture ( ) 　　b. 円滑な社会的関係
3. smooth social relationship ( ) 　c. 気分を害する
4. social rank and status ( ) 　　d. 前後関係や状況を考慮した
5. ping-pong style of conversation ( ) 　e. 社会的地位と威信
6. mutual connections ( ) 　　f. 互いの関係
7. tempura metaphor ( ) 　　g. てんぷらにたとえる
8. get offended ( ) 　　　　h. 調整する
9. contextual ( ) 　　　　i. 同質の文化
10. modify ( ) 　　　　　j. ピンポンのような会話のやりとり

39

READING

When we communicate face to face, we bring with us the social and cultural values of our society. Our culture influences our communication style — the words we use and the way we speak. For instance, North American speech is "friendly" while Japanese speech is "respectful." The United States is a nation of immigrants. Originally, people did not come from the same cultural background, so it was necessary to be "friendly" in order to live together and set up a country. Japan is a homogenous culture. People come from the same ethnic group, speak the same language and share one common culture. The important thing is to maintain smooth social relationships. People use different levels of polite language depending on the other person's social rank and status.

Another important social difference is that in the United States, the focus is on the individual, while in Japan, the focus is on the group. This affects people's conversation styles. Generally, North Americans emphasize the right of the individual to express him or herself. The focus of speech is on the "I" — on the speaker — and what he or she wants to say. In this sense, American speech is individualistic. North American speech also uses the "ping-pong" style of conversation. This means the listener immediately "throws back" comments and ideas right after the speaker has finished talking. The speaker and listener have a direct exchange of information.

In contrast, in Japan, where people value mutual connections and social relationship, speech is very indirect. The communication style of the Japanese can be described by the "tempura metaphor." In Japan, it is sometimes hard to understand what the speaker is trying to say. One can get to the main point only after removing the coating of the "tempura." Furthermore, people avoid direct statements so that the listener does not get offended. The focus of speech is on the emotional condition of the listener and the situation. This is called the contextual style of communication. On the other hand, the listener is expected to understand the message by guessing "intuitively" what the speaker is trying to say. This difference between the Japanese and North American communication styles has been observed in many business situations.

Chapter 6 Culture and Communication Style

Japanese and North Americans are not the only groups of people with contrasting communication styles. People all over the world have different conversation patterns. People of one culture will tend to talk a lot, interrupt conversations frequently, and talk more quickly and louder than people of another culture. They want to participate actively in the discussion. Meanwhile, people from other cultures prefer to speak less, listen more, and refrain from interrupting the speaker. The listener shows respect to the speaker by giving feedback only after the speaker has finished.

Differences in communication styles can cause miscommunication problems, so it is sometimes safe to modify your communication style according to your conversation partner.

EXERCISES

A New words

Circle the letter that gives the correct meaning of the underlined words/phrases.

1. Communication style in the passage refers to
   a. the way people speak.
   b. the words people choose.
   c. the words people choose and the way they speak.

2. The U.S. is a nation of immigrants means that originally
   a. people lived together.
   b. people came from various cultural backgrounds.
   c. people chose to work hard.

3. Japan is a homogenous culture because
   a. people eat the same food.
   b. people belong to the same culture.
   c. people come from different cultures.

4. To guess intuitively what the speaker is saying means
   a. ask the speaker what he or she wants to say.
   b. pretend you understand.
   c. imagine what the speaker is saying.

5. In daily conversations, when someone refrains from giving feedback, he
   a. speaks less and listens more.
   b. speaks more and listens less.
   c. speaks less and asks questions.

6. When you offend someone, you
   a. hurt his/her feelings.
   b. hurt him/her physically.
   c. hurt him/her by shouting.

7. To modify your communication style, you need to
   a. completely change your way of speaking.
   b. maintain your speaking style.
   c. adjust your speaking style.

B Read for the main ideas

Choose the answer that best completes the meaning of the sentence.

1. According to the passage, the way we talk and use words is influenced by
   a. our personality.
   b. our family.
   c. our culture.

2. According to the passage, American speech is
   a. friendly and individualistic.
   b. polite and socially conscious.
   c. fast and hard to understand.

3. According to the passage, Japanese speech is generally
   a. polite and very direct.
   b. polite and individualistic.
   c. polite and very indirect.

4. In "ping pong" conversations,
   a. it is hard to understand what the speaker is saying.
   b. people exchange a lot of information.
   c. the speaker and listener are polite to each other.

Chapter 6 Culture and Communication Style

5. Japanese speech can be described by the "tempura metaphor" because
   a. it is hard to understand what the speaker is saying.
   b. people exchange a lot of information.
   c. it is direct and very polite.

6. In some cultures, people ask questions and interrupt during conversations because
   a. they want to speak more.
   b. they want to listen more.
   c. they want to participate actively in the discussion.

7. In some cultures, people do not talk too much in dialogues because
   a. they want to speak more.
   b. they want to listen more.
   c. they want to show respect to the speaker.

C Read for details

Choose the answer that best completes the meaning of the sentence.

1. In daily conversations, Japanese use different levels of polite language
   a. according to their father's social rank and status.
   b. according to the mood of the speaker.
   c. according to the social rank and status of the other person.

2. Because American speech focuses on the "I", or the speaker, it
   a. is called polite speech.
   b. is called individualistic.
   c. is called democratic.

3. In daily conversations, Japanese usually focus on the
   a. emotional condition of the speaker.
   b. emotional condition of the listener.
   c. emotional condition of the situation and the listener.

4. People try to avoid direct statements in Japan because they
   a. do not want to offend the other person.
   b. do not want to talk too much.

43

c. do not want to listen too long.

5. According to the third paragraph, in daily conversations in Japan, the listener must
   a. try to imagine what the speaker is trying to say.
   b. try to understand the accent of the speaker.
   c. try to understand the emotional condition of the speaker.

D Read between the lines

Choose the word/phrase that best connects the meanings of the sentence pair.

1. 1) Our culture influences our communication style.
   2) Our culture affects the words we use and the manner in which we speak.
      a. in other words   b. for example   c. similarly

2. 1) In the U.S., people did not come from the same cultural background.
   2) Japanese people have the same cultural background.
      a. for example   b. in contrast   c. similarly

3. 1) North Americans emphasize the right of the individual to express himself/herself.
   2) When two people talk, the speaker focuses on what he/she wants to say.
      a. however   b. finally   c. therefore

4. 1) In other cultures, the listener does not interrupt, and gives positive feedback.
   2) The listener wants to show respect to the speaker.
      a. for example   b. because   c. in contrast

5. 1) In Japan, mutual connections and social relationships are important.
   2) The communication style is very indirect.
      a. as a result   b. however   c. in contrast

Chapter 6 Culture and Communication Style

E Cloze listening

Fill in the gaps with words/phrases from below. Then, listen to the recording and check your answers.

1. participate actively   2. conversation patterns   3. very indirect
4. by guessing   5. positive feedback   6. express himself
7. direct statements   8. throws   9. the speaker   10. main point

People's ways of thinking and their cultural values influence their use of language. In Japan, mutual connections and social relationships are very important. Thus the conversation style is a_____. The communication style of the Japanese can also be described by the "tempura metaphor." It is hard to
5 understand what the speaker is trying to say. One can get to the b_____ only after removing the coating of the "tempura." Furthermore, people avoid c_____ in order not to offend the listener. The listener is expected to understand the message d_____ what the speaker is trying to say.

In the United States, the right of the individual to e_____ is very
10 important. Therefore, the focus of speech is on f_____ and what he wants to say. The communication style of North American speech is also called the "ping-pong" conversation style. This means the listener immediately g_____ comments and ideas right after the speaker has finished talking. The speaker and listener engage in a direct exchange of information.

15 People all over the world have different h_____. Some people tend to talk more, interrupt conversations more, and talk more quickly and louder than others. They want to i_____ in the discussion. Meanwhile, people from other cultures prefer to speak less, listen more, and give j_____ to the other person. The listener shows respect to the speaker by refraining from
20 giving feedback, and listening more. Differences in communication style can cause miscommunication problems, so it is sometimes a good idea to adjust your communication style to suit that of the other person.

45

ICC Activity

Check your communication style.

What would you say/do in the following situations? Choose a, b, or c.

1) Your friend invites you to a party, but you have a report to finish.
    a. I'm sorry, I can't.   b. Thank you.
    c. Sure, I will come (but you don't).

2) Your best friend cut his/her hair differently, and she looks strange.
    a. Tell him/her the truth.   b. Say her hairstyle is good.
    c. Say he/she should look for a better beauty parlor.

3) You disagree with what another student is saying.
    a. Tell him/her you disagree.   b. Ask questions.   c. Keep quiet.

4) Your friend is not talking to you.
    a. Ask him/her what's wrong.   b. Wait and ask later.
    c. Worry but say nothing.

Add your scores: a=3 points / b=2 points / c =1 point
What your score means:

More than 8 points	You are very direct. Try to listen more.
5-7 points	You speak out sometimes, but usually choose not to do so. Try to be more honest.
4-1 points	You are very indirect. Try to speak out more.

Chapter 7 Self-disclosure

"To whom does one speak or not speak? About what may one talk or not talk? How completely is inner experience shared or withheld? Answering these questions will help you understand human relationships." (Barnlund, 1975)

「自分について誰に話すか、何を話すか、内的体験をどの程度深く話すか話さないか。このような質問に答えることは、人間関係を理解するのに役立つ」

Warm-up

Look at the following pictures and answer the question below.

Q picture 1 Which person do you think is more open and friendly?
picture 2 Do you think these people will become friends?

Key words

Match the words in the left column with their meaning in the right column. This will help you understand the reading passage.

1. initial greeting （　）　　　a. 相手
2. general topic （　）　　　　b. 一般的な話題
3. acquaintance （　）　　　　c. 意味深く
4. self-disclosure （　）　　　d. 経済的な
5. religion （　）　　　　　　e. 最初の挨拶
6. financial （　）　　　　　　f. 自己開示
7. opposite （　）　　　　　　g. 宗教
8. stranger （　）　　　　　　h. 初対面の人
9. significantly （　）　　　　i. 知人
10. counterpart （　）　　　　j. 反対の
11. secretive （　）　　　　　k. 秘密主義の
12. defensive （　）　　　　　l. 防衛的な

READING

When you meet someone for the first time, how do you decide whether or not you want to be friends with him/her? Usually, after the initial greeting you start to exchange information, first on general topics, and gradually you move on to more specific topics, such as your hobbies, your skills and your interests. At this stage of the interaction you feel either that you want to know more about the other person, or you lose interest. By exchanging information about one another, you decide to become friends with the other person, or simply remain acquaintances.

The act of talking about yourself to the other person is called self-disclosure. Everybody discloses things about themselves, but what people say, to whom they talk, and how much information they reveal about themselves is influenced by culture.

Dean Barnlund studied self-disclosure among Japanese college students and compared it with that of American college students. He asked the students to indicate how deeply they express their opinions on several topics. The topics included hobbies, personal interests and taste in food, music, movies, their feelings about their body, and other serious topics such as religion, financial situation, and personality. He also asked them how often they talk about these topics to their mother, father, to a friend of the same sex, a friend of the opposite sex, other acquaintances, and strangers.

He found that both Japanese and Americans were similar in the topics they disclosed and to whom they disclosed. But Barnlund found out that Japanese and American students differed significantly on how deeply they disclosed information about themselves. Japanese students disclosed less than American students.

It is interesting to see what happens when a person who usually discloses a lot (person A), and a person who usually discloses very little (person B), interact with one another. Person A may talk about his/her feelings, thoughts, and opinions freely without being asked. He will expect his counterpart to do the same. However, person B will not reveal much about himself easily. He will wait until he is asked. Even so, he may not say anything about himself. In this kind of interaction, person A, by talking a lot about himself, may feel that person B is secretive or overly shy or defensive. On the other hand, person B may feel that the other person is overly self-expressive, pushy, and self-centered.

Differences in personality probably account for many of these tensions. But the situation is more difficult when people from different cultural backgrounds meet. For example, in Japan, people are not expected to disclose too much at the first meeting. Japanese take time to disclose information. That is their custom. Japanese are often surprised when they hear Americans talk too much at the first meeting. Japanese feel pressured and may even judge the American as being too aggressive. It is important to be aware of the self-disclosure practice of other people in order to understand them better.

EXERCISES

A New words

Circle the letter that gives the correct meaning of the underlined words/phrases.

1. Typical general topics are
   a. weather and climate.   b. hobbies and interests.   c. special skills.

2. An acquaintance is someone you
   a. have met but don't know much about.   b. can call a friend.   c. avoid.

3. A secretive person usually tells you
   a. a lot about himself.   b. a lot about other people.   c. very little.

4. Becoming defensive means
   a. becoming friendly.   b. trying to protect oneself.   c. attacking.

5. "He gives the impression that he is aggressive" means
   a. he looks shy.   b. he looks thoughtful.   c. he looks excited.

B Read for the main ideas

Choose the answer that best completes the meaning of the sentence.

1. Self-disclosure is

a. talking about someone to others.
  b. talking about yourself to others.
  c. not talking about yourself to others.

2. Self-disclosure is uniquely
   a. American behavior.
   b. Japanese behavior.
   c. human behavior.

3. Dean Barnlund studied self-disclosure of
   a. Japanese and American business persons.
   b. Japanese and American students.
   c. Japanese and American children.

4. Dean Barnlund found that the Japanese level of self-disclosure
   a. was deeper than Americans'.
   b. was of the same depth.
   c. was not as deep as Americans'.

5. Japanese often find American disclosure
   a. a bit aggressive.
   b. a bit shy.
   c. a bit secretive.

C Read for details

Choose the answer that best completes the meaning of the sentence.

1. When we meet for the first time, we usually start by talking about
   a. specific matters.   b. general matters.   c. private matters.

2. Then we move on to more personal matters such as
   a. our hobbies.   b. the weather.   c. world news.

3. Self-disclosure is the act of
   a. asking personal questions.
   b. disclosing secrets about oneself.
   c. speaking about oneself.

Chapter 7 Self-disclosure

4. Barnlund found that compared to Japanese, Americans disclosed
    a. more information.   b. less information.   c. far less information.

5. Judging from the way Japanese talk about themselves, Americans may think that Japanese are
    a. open.   b. aggressive.   c. defensive.

6. When cultural backgrounds differ, we must
    a. be careful in making personality judgments based on self-disclosure.
    b. make quick judgments of others' personalities.
    c. disclose as little as we can to avoid misunderstanding.

D Read between the lines

Choose the word/phrase that best connects the meanings of the sentence pair.

1. 1) When you meet for the first time, you start by exchanging greetings.
   2) You move on to exchanging information.
      a. when   b. then   c. so

2. 1) Everybody discloses things about themselves.
   2) Culture influences when and how people disclose.
      a. as   b. so   c. but

3. 1) Barnlund asked students to indicate how deeply they disclosed information about different topics.
   2) Religion, tastes, financial situation, and personality.
      a. such as   b. as   c. in addition

4. 1) Usually people disclose more to people with whom they feel close.
   2) They will disclose more to a friend than to a stranger.
      a. however   b. for example   c. on top of that

5. 1) Usually people who disclose a lot expect their counterpart to do the same.
   2) If their counterpart is a shy person, he will not disclose much.
      a. so   b. consequently   c. however

E Cloze listening

Fill in the gaps with words/phrases from below. Then, listen to the recording and check your answers.

1. differed   2. stage   3. general   4. self-disclosure   5. greeting
6. serious   7. specific   8. less   9. influenced   10. express

When you meet someone for the first time, how do you find out whether you want to be friends with him/her? Usually, after the ritual of a_____ you start to exchange information, first on b_____ topics and gradually you move on to more c_____ topics, such as your hobbies, your skills and
5 your interests. At this d_____ of the interaction you feel either you want to know more about the other person, or you feel you don't want to know more about him. By exchanging information about one another, you decide to become friends with the other person, or stay as acquaintances.

The act of speaking about yourself to another person is called e_____.
10 Everybody discloses things about themselves, but what to say, whom to talk to and to what extent one discloses is f_____ by culture.

Dean Barnlund studied self-disclosure among Japanese college students and compared it with that of American college students. He asked the students to indicate how deeply they g_____ their opinions on several topics. The
15 topics included hobbies, personal interests and taste in food, music, movies, and other h_____ topics like religion, financial situation, and personality. He also asked them how often they talk about these topics to their mother, father, to a friend of the same sex, a friend of the opposite sex, other acquaintances, and strangers. He found out that Japanese and Americans were similar in what topics
20 they disclose to whom, but i_____ significantly on how deeply they disclosed about themselves. The Japanese level of disclosure was j_____ than the American level.

Chapter 7 Self-disclosure

ICC Activity

A   You meet someone for the first time in a party. Which of the following topics will you talk about? Put a check on your choice.

	Yes	No
1) about the weather	_____	_____
2) about his/her clothes	_____	_____
3) about your future dream	_____	_____
4) about your family	_____	_____
5) about the food	_____	_____
6) about movies/music	_____	_____
7) about your friends	_____	_____
8) about your boy/girl friend	_____	_____
9) about your hometown	_____	_____
10) about sports	_____	_____

B   In group of four, each person take turns talking about the following topics.

1) your happiest moments
2) what I am interested in right now
3) what I am most concerned about
4) your unhappiest moments
5) the problems I am facing now
6) your thoughts for the future
7) a pressing personal issue

Chapter 8　Self-assertiveness

"Communication is direct, honest and open." (Stewart, 1975)
「コミュニケーションは直接的で、正直で率直である」

Warm-up

What would you do in the following situation? Choose from 1 to 4.

Your friend is saying something. You disagree with him.

1　2 　3 　4

1) You say, "Your ideas are good, but …"
2) You keep quiet and listen attentively.
3) You tell your friend to stop talking.
4) You leave the room.

Key words

Match the words in the left column with their meaning in the right column. This will help you understand the reading passage.

1. read *one's* mind (　　)　　a. 行間を読む
2. read between the lines (　　)　　b. 結果
3. assertive (　　)　　c. 行動の変化
4. self-assertiveness (　　)　　d. 食物の包装
5. describe the situation (　　)　　e. 状況を描写する
6. outcome (　　)　　f. 積極的な
7. food wrapping (　　)　　g. 積極的に自分を表現すること
8. accuse (　　)　　h. 責める
9. behavioral change (　　)　　i. 相互依存
10. interdependence (　　)　　j. 人の考えや気持ちを推し量る

READING

When cultural backgrounds differ we need to express our thoughts and feelings to be understood. We cannot expect the other person to read our minds or read between the lines. So we need to express our thoughts and feelings in a clear and positive manner. And we need to continue to communicate until the other person gets the message. In other words, we need to be assertive. Self-assertiveness means expressing our thoughts, opinions and feelings while respecting others. It means direct, honest and open communication.

How can people be self-assertive? Sharon and Gordon Bower say "to assert yourself effectively, four things are necessary: describe the situation, express your feeling toward it, specify what you think has to be done, and state the outcome or consequence." Imagine that you are a leader of a weekly meeting of your school's English Speaking Society. The meeting is held during lunchtime in a classroom, so students bring their own lunch. Since everyone has to rush to their next class after the meeting, very often, plastic bottles and food wrappings are left behind. You have to clean up every time. Now, you want everyone to take care of their own trash. How would you assert yourself to the members?

The first step is to describe the situation; get everyone to have a common understanding of the problem. You can say, "Every week after our meeting, there is trash left on the desks. Since the room must be clean for the next class, I have been cleaning up each week for a month now." The important thing here is not to accuse anyone, but to get people to see the problem.

The second step is to express your feelings about the situation. You can say, "I know everybody is in a rush to go to their next class, but it is very frustrating to clean up after everyone leaves. I was even late for my next class last week." The point here is not to blame anyone for the irresponsible behavior, but to say how you honestly feel about the situation.

The third step is to express specifically the behavioral change you want. You can

say, "We should not leave any trash in the room. Make sure to throw away your trash. I would appreciate it if each one would double check that nothing is left behind."
Specific description of the desired behavior is important especially in intercultural groups.

The fourth step is to express the possible outcome. You can say, "If we all share the responsibility and clean up, no one will be late for their next class. That way, I will feel much happier about our weekly meetings."

In some cultures, it is hard to be assertive because people have strong interdependence. In other cultures, people are assertive because each person thinks he or she is independent. Japanese students should know how to be assertive when talking with people from other cultures.

EXERCISES

A New Words

Circle the letter that gives the correct meaning of the underlined words/phrases.

1. In the passage, when cultural backgrounds differ
   a. people come from different cultures.
   b. people come from the same culture.
   c. people come from unknown cultures.

2. An assertive person
   a. hides his thoughts and feelings.
   b. expresses his thoughts and feelings.
   c. is the leader of a group.

3. Which phrase means the same as consequence?
   a. Thoughts and feelings.
   b. Doing something.
   c. An outcome or result.

4. You blame someone when you
   a. tell him to clean the floor.
   b. tell him that he did something good.

c. tell him he did something irresponsible.

5. "There was <u>trash</u> in the room" means
   a. students were eating their lunch.
   b. students were rushing to their classroom.
   c. plastic bottles and food wrappings were on the desks or lying on the floor.

B Read for the main ideas

Choose the answer that best completes the meaning of the sentence.

1. According to the passage, we have to express ourselves clearly because
   a. the other person can't read our minds.
   b. the other person is very positive.
   c. the other person can read our minds.

2. According to the passage, to communicate assertively
   a. we need to express our feelings.
   b. we need to blame others.
   c. we need to accuse people around us.

3. If you are a leader and there is a problem, the first thing you must do is
   a. to tell everyone what the problem is.
   b. to hide your feelings about it.
   c. to tell the teacher there is a problem.

4. In some cultures, it is hard to be assertive because
   a. people are very responsible.
   b. people have strong interdependence.
   c. people are very independent.

C Read for details

Choose the answer that best completes the meaning of the sentence.

1. According to the passage, when you describe the situation, you must
   a. be emotinal.

    b. make sure everybody understands the problem.
    c. rush to the classroom.

2. When you express your feelings about the situation or the problem,
    a. you must be honest.
    b. you must blame others for the problem.
    c. you must be angry.

3. The third step, "specify the behavioral change you want", means
    a. to explain what you want others to do.
    b. to explain what others should bring to the meeting.
    c. to explain the cause of the problem.

4. When each person thinks he is independent,
    a. it is easy to be interdependent.
    b. it is easy to be self-assertive.
    c. it is hard to be self-assertive.

5. What should Japanese students do when talking to foreigners?
    a. They should be more friendly.
    b. They should be more interdependent.
    c. They should be more self-assertive.

D Read between the lines

Choose the word/phrase that best connects the meanings of the sentence pair.

1. 1) Everyone left their trash in the room.
   2) I had to clean up.
       a. therefore   b. surprisingly   c. in addition

2. 1) I was late for my next class.
   2) I had to clean up after everyone had left.
       a. therefore   b. because   c. suddenly

3. 1) In some countries, it is easy to be self-assertive.
   2) In other countries, it is hard to express your thoughts and feelings.
       a. because   b. furthermore   c. but

Chapter 8 Self-assertiveness

4. 1) Make sure you throw away your trash.
   2) You can't join the meeting.
         a. but   b. in contrast   c. otherwise

5. 1) Students have to be self-assertive.
   2) They should express themselves better.
         a. in other words   b. otherwise   c. by contrast

E Cloze listening

Fill in the gaps with words/phrases from below. Then, listen to the recording and check your answers.

> 1. desired   2. outcome   3. describe   4. common   5. feeling
> 6. accuse   7. respecting   8. expressing   9. specify
> 10. irresponsible

Students and workers need to express their thoughts and feelings, and be self-assertive. Self-assertion means a_____ our thoughts, opinions and feelings while b_____ others.

How can people be self-assertive? Sharon and Gordon Bower say "to assert
5 yourself effectively, four things are necessary: c_____ the situation, express your d_____ toward it, e_____ what you think has to be done, and state the f_____ or consequence."

The first step is to describe the situation; get everyone to have a g_____ understanding of the problem. The important thing here is not to h_____
10 anyone, but to get people to see the problem. The second step is to express your feelings about the situation. The point here is not to blame anyone for the i_____ behavior, but to say how you honestly feel about the situation. The third step is to express specifically the behavioral change you want. Specific description of the j_____ behavior is important, especially in
15 intercultural groups. The fourth step is to express the possible outcome.

59

ICC Activity

A What would you do/say in the following situations?

1) Your friend is smoking in the room and you didn't like it.
2) You found out that the CD you bought does not work.
3) Your friend has been asking you to pay for his/her juice at a restaurant.
4) You have a roommate. She cooks every day and watches TV every day until midnight. You have to share (50%) of the electric and gas bills every month.
5) You have a test tomorrow, and your friend gives you a phone call. She wants to talk about her problems.

B Choose the assertive communication style for the following case.

  Your friend often calls you when you are doing your homework. You tell him/her that you are doing your homework but he/she keeps on talking for at least an hour and doesn't let you hang up. You want him/her to let you hang up without accusing you of being unfriendly.

1) Describe the situation:
   a. I often get a call from you in the evening.
   b. You always call me at inconvenient hours.
2) Express your feeling:
   a. I think you are inconsiderate. Why can't you think about how I feel?
   b. Sometimes I can't finish my homework because we talk for hours and I feel quite uneasy about that.
3) Specify the behavior you desire:
   a. I want you to be more considerate of my needs.
   b. Could you make the call short and let me hang up when I'm doing my homework?
4) Outcome:
   a. I'd appreciate your consideration and feel much better about our relationship.
   b. If you keep on doing this to me, I won't answer your calls in the evening.

Chapter 9 Active Listening

"Communication is a two-way traffic: both speaker and listener are active at the same time." (Hartley, 1999)

「コミュニケーションは双方通行である。話し手も聞き手も同時に能動的である」

Warm-up

Answer the following question.

You have a complicated problem at your part-time job. You decide to talk to your friend to get some advice. You have just started to explain the problem. Your friend cuts you off by saying, "Okay, I understand the problem. I advise you to do so and so."

Q
1. Do you think your friend really listened to you?
2. Do you think your friend really understood the problem?
3. Do you think his advice is useful?
4. Will you follow his advice?

Key words

Match the words in the left column with their meaning in the right column. This will help you understand the reading passage.

1. back-channeling (　　)   a. あいづち
2. good listener (　　)   b. 相手に確認してもらう
3. check(ing) with the other person (　　)   c. 明らかに
4. verbalize (　　)   d. 言い換えること
5. interpretation (　　)   e. 意図した内容
6. paraphrasing (　　)   f. 公の場での放送
7. intended message (　　)   g. 解釈
8. positive (　　)   h. 肯定的な
9. public announcement (　　)   i. ことばに出して言う
10. obviously (　　)   j. 良い聞き手

READING

As a people, the Japanese generally are quiet and reserved. In meetings and discussions, they tend to listen more often than speak up. They use frequent back-channeling — *aizuchi* — and expressions like *sou-desu-ne* in conversations. To a foreigner, this seems as if the Japanese is agreeing with the other person. Actually this simply means that the Japanese heard what the speaker has said. Does all this mean that Japanese are good listeners who really understand what they hear?

To be a good listener means to be an active listener. Active listening is very important in conversations, especially in intercultural communication. It is not easy for people of different cultural backgrounds to understand each other. They have different ways of thinking, feeling, and expressing themselves. Active listening involves checking with the other person to confirm if you correctly understood the message you heard. To do this you need to verbalize your interpretation of what you heard. This means asking questions, or repeating or paraphrasing what the other person said. By doing this, the speaker can check if the listener received the intended message.

Let me share my experience. Two French friends of mine came to Tokyo for the first time. They went sightseeing and shopping, and when they came back, they told me their impressions of Tokyo. Their impressions were very positive except for one thing, the noise on the trains. Surprised, I responded, "You find trains noisy? Yes, some people talk too loudly, especially high school students."

They said, "Oh no, not that. It's the announcements, the constant public announcements. There are very few quiet moments. How can people stand it?"

At first, I misinterpreted their comments but they could correct me because I used active listening. For my part, I explained that inside the trains the announcements are very helpful and necessary so that people can get off at the right place.

"Oh really! So people rely on those announcements," they said, surprised. Obviously, people who do not understand Japanese think the announcements are unnecessary. For them, it's just noise.

If I had responded to their comment about the noisy trains by just saying *sou-desu-*

Chapter 9 Active Listening

ne, they would have gone away thinking that I found public announcements noisy, just as they did. I would have gone away thinking that my friends didn't like people talking loudly on the trains. But because I used an active listening technique, we were able to correct each other's misunderstanding.

Active listening is one way to show that you are interested in what the other person is saying, and that you really want to understand the message. As a result, it keeps you from judging the other person based on your own values and ways of doing things. It shows your respect, and this is highly appreciated by the speaker. Active listening is one way to show that your mind is open to what the other person has to say. It is an effective means of bringing people closer. When people feel closer, they lower their defenses and begin to disclose more.

Finally, active listening is not the same as agreeing with the other person. It is a behavior that comes from a sincere desire to build respect and a positive relationship.

EXERCISES

A New words

Circle the letter that gives the correct meaning of the underlined words/phrases.

1. When you <u>agree with</u> someone,
    a. you think the same way.
    b. you think differently.
    c. you give your ideas about something.

2. "You need to <u>verbalize</u> your ideas" means
    a. you need to think about the other person's ideas.
    b. you need to think about your ideas.
    c. you need to say your ideas.

3. The listener understood the speaker's <u>intended</u> message means
    a. the listener understood what the speaker did not want to say.
    b. the listener heard what the speaker was saying.
    c. the listener understood what the speaker wanted to say.

4. The <u>constant</u> public announcements in the train means
   a. the passengers are talking all the time.
   b. the students are noisy.
   c. it is rarely quiet in the train.

5. When you <u>rely on</u> someone, that means
   a. he/she is important to you
   b. he/she is a rich person.
   c. he/she is a polite person.

B Read for the main ideas

Choose the answer that best completes the meaning of the sentence.

1. Foreigners usually think the Japanese always agree with others because
   a. they always smile.
   b. they do frequent back-channeling.
   c. they always ask questions.

2. Active listening means
   a. you check if the speaker understood you.
   b. you check with the speaker if other people understood you.
   c. you check with the speaker to see if you understood his message.

3. The public announcements are necessary because
   a. they help people get off the train quickly.
   b. they help people get on the bus on time.
   c. they help people get off at the right station.

4. Active listening is important because
   a. it helps you deny what the other person is saying.
   b. it helps you become closer to the other person.
   c. it helps you get useless information about the person.

5. When people feel close to each other, they usually
   a. begin shopping together.
   b. start debating political issues.
   c. begin to talk about themselves.

Chapter 9 Active Listening

C Read for details

Choose the answer that best completes the meaning of the sentence.

1. It is hard for people from different cultures to understand each other because
   a. they feel, think and talk differently.
   b. they understand the correct messages very quickly.
   c. they believe that their country is the best.

2. The two friends from France have
   a. few good impressions of Tokyo.
   b. mostly negative impressions of Tokyo.
   c. mostly good impressions of Tokyo.

3. Foreigners think the public announcements are noisy because
   a. they do not understand English.
   b. they do not understand Japanese.
   c. they do not talk in the trains.

4. The writer used an active listening technique by
   a. paraphrasing.
   b. objecting.
   c. changing the topic.

5. When you show respect to the speaker through active listening,
   a. the speaker feels happy about it.
   b. the speaker feels you are judging him/her.
   c. the speaker thinks you are noisy.

D Read between the lines

Choose the word/phrase that best connects the meanings of the sentence pair.

1. 1) When the Japanese say "*sou-desu-ne*," the foreigner thinks he is agreeing.
   2) The Japanese is saying he heard what the speaker has said.
      a. similarly   b. actually   c. in addition

2. 1) It is not easy for people from different cultural backgrounds to understand each other.

65

2) They have different ways of thinking, feeling, and talking.
   a. therefore   b. because   c. however

3. 1) My friends first thought public announcements were noisy.
   2) I used active listening and I was able to make them understand.
      a. but   b. unfortunately   c. therefore

4. 1) In active listening, you show you are interested in the speaker.
   2) He feels happy about it.
      a. but   b. as a result   c. however

5. 1) In active listening, you show that you have an open mind.
   2) It is an effective means for bringing people closer together.
      a. unfortunately   b. however   c. in addition

E Cloze listening

Fill in the gaps with words/phrases from below. Then, listen to the recording and check your answers.

1. appreciated   2. good listeners   3. to understand
4. intended message   5. interested   6. to respect   7. closer
8. agreeing   9. correctly   10. asking questions

Japanese generally are quiet and reserved. This does not mean they are a_____. In conversations, they use frequent back channeling – *aizuchi* – and expressions like *sou-desu-ne*. To a foreigner, this means the Japanese is b_____. Actually this simply means that the Japanese heard what the
5 speaker has said.
   To be a good listener means to be an active listener. Active listening is very important in conversations, especially in intercultural communication. It is not easy for people with different cultural backgrounds c_____ each other. They have different ways of thinking, feeling, and expressing themselves. Active listening
10 involves checking with the other person if you understood d_____ the

66

Chapter 9 Active Listening

message you heard. To do this you need to verbalize your interpretation of what you heard. This means e_____, repeating or paraphrasing what the other person said. By doing this, the speaker can check if you understood his f_____.

15   Active listening is one way to show that you are g_____ in what the other person is saying, and that you really want to understand the message. It keeps you from judging the other person based on your own values and ways of doing things. It shows your respect, and this is highly h_____ by the speaker. Active listening is one way to show your mind is open to what the other
20   person has to say. It is an effective means of bringing people i_____. Finally, active listening does not mean simply agreeing with the other person. It is a behavior that comes from a sincere desire j_____ and to build a positive relationship.

ICC Activity

In pairs, practice active listening for five minutes each. Choose one topic from below and take turns talking. Listen to your partner and repeat or paraphrase the main points of what he/she says. The partner will check whether you understood correctly and restate if there is any misunderstanding. You can do it in English or Japanese.

Topics 1) Why I like [don't like] sports.
2) Why I think English is important.
3) Is global warming an important issue?

Chapter 10 Conflict Management

"Five communication behaviors that occur during negotiation are attacking, evading, informing, opening, and uniting." (Raider and Coleman, 2000)

「交渉に見られるコミュニケーション行動は、攻撃、逃避、情報提供、心を開かせること、問題を共有すること、の5つである」

Warm-up

Think about the following situation.

You are the leader of a swimming club. Every week the group has a practice from 5 p.m. to 7 p.m. The club members do not come on time; they come 30 minutes late, or sometimes they do not come at all. What will you do?

Key words

Match the words in the left column with their meaning in the right column. This will help you understand the reading passage.

1. conflict (　　)
2. attacking (　　)
3. evading (　　)
4. informing (　　)
5. uniting (　　)
6. illustrate (　　)
7. administration (　　)
8. sanitation (　　)
9. profitable (　　)
10. elaborate (　　)

a. 衛生
b. 問題を共有する
c. 詳しく述べる
d. 攻撃
e. 事務局
f. 情報提供
g. 逃避
h. 紛争、対立
i. 例証する
j. 利益が出る

READING

In intercultural situations, conflicts caused by misunderstanding abound. Raider and Coleman say people use five communication styles in a conflict situation. These are:
5 attacking, evading, informing, opening, and uniting (AEIOU). Let's see how Kazuko, a Japanese college student, and Tom, an American exchange student, illustrate these communication styles.

10 Tom and Kazuko belong to the same after-class school club. The group is discussing their plan for the school festival. Tom comes up with a lot of ideas; Kazuko keeps quiet.

Tom: Kazuko, don't you have any brain in your head?

Kazuko: You don't know anything. You just talk like a machine gun!

In the above interaction, both Tom and Kazuko are attacking each other. By attacking,
15 negative feeling towards each other builds up. This kind of communication is destructive.

What about this response?

Tom: Kazuko, what do you think of a *yakitori* stand for the school festival?

Kazuko: Sorry Tom. I've got to go to class now.

20 In this situation, Kazuko is using evasion. This will leave Tom very uneasy and anxious for support.

What if Kazuko responded to Tom's question in the following way?

Kazuko: Well, a *yakitori* stand is a good idea. But we have to get special permission from the administration. They are very strict about sanitation. I don't think we're
25 allowed to handle raw meat.

This time, Kazuko is using the informing style. The information she provides is helpful. Tom will feel that she is a reliable member of the school festival project.

Kazuko may respond yet in a different way.

Kazuko: You want to do a *yakitori* stand. Tell me more about your idea.

30 *Tom:* I think we can attract many people, young and old. We can sell it cheap and make money for our club.

Kazuko: You think yakitori is popular with everybody and that it is profitable. I get your point.

This interaction shows Kazuko is using the opening style. She is open to Tom's idea and encourages him to elaborate on his idea. By doing so, two main points become clear: the food stand needs to attract many customers and it has to be profitable.

The next type is the uniting style.

Kazuko: Okay, let's think of a way to clear the sanitation requirement and at the same time set up a stand that's attractive to everybody and that is profitable.

Tom: Well, if we can't handle raw meat, maybe we can get precooked *yakitori* and grill it at the stand. We can make hotdogs too.

Kazuko: Precooked *yakitori* is not a bad idea.

In the above interaction, Kazuko is using the uniting style. She is addressing both her concern and Tom's concern. By joining their efforts they come up with a satisfying solution.

In a conflict situation, we need to take extra time to inform the other person, be open to new ideas, and unite people's ideas. Conflicts caused by misinterpretation and misunderstanding can be avoided or overcome by using the informing, opening, and uniting (IOU) styles of communication.

EXERCISES

A New Words

Circle the letter that gives the correct meaning of the underlined words/phrases.

1. According to the passage, to illustrate means
    a. to give an example.
    b. to give directions.
    c. to become friends.

2. Attacking is destructive in a relationship because
    a. it makes people become friends.
    b. it makes people communicate better.
    c. it makes people dislike each other.

3. Selling yakitori is profitable because

Chapter 10 Conflict Management

      a. it will make people happy.

      b. it will make a lot of money.

      c. it will make students work hard.

4. When you <u>elaborate</u> on your idea,

      a. you explain more about what you said.

      b. you ask more questions.

      c. you listen more.

5. According to the passage, <u>precooked</u> yakitori means

      a. raw.

      b. fresh.

      c. cooked beforehand.

B Read for the main ideas

Choose the answer that best completes the meaning of the sentence.

1. According to the passage, when there is conflict, people usually

      a. use all of the five communication styles.

      b. use some of the five communication styles.

      c. use one of the five communication styles.

2. Attacking is destructive to people because

      a. people develop negative feelings towards each other.

      b. people build up positive feelings towards each other.

      c. people start to work hard together.

3. According to the passage, when people use the informing style

      a. they give more and new information about the topic.

      b. they attract many people to their project.

      c. they become more negative.

4. When the speakers make an effort to find a solution to the problem together,

      a. they use the informing style.

      b. they use the uniting style.

      c. they use the opening style.

5. Misunderstanding can be avoided by
   a. using the AEIOU communication styles.
   b. using the AEU communication styles.
   c. using the IOU communication styles.

C Read for details

Choose the answer that best completes the meaning of the sentence.

1. According to the passage, people use AEIOU when
   a. there is a school festival.
   b. there is a happy occasion.
   c. there is a conflict situation.

2. In the passage, Tom and Kazuko were
   a. discussing plans for the school festival.
   b. debating about the school festival.
   c. discussing plans for travel.

3. In the dialog, Tom felt very uneasy because
   a. Kazuko tried to avoid school.
   b. Kazuko tried to avoid his question.
   c. Kazuko tried to avoid the school festival.

4. Tom thinks that when they sell things for a cheap price,
   a. they will get more help from people.
   b. they will lose money.
   c. they will attract many people.

5. IOU means
   a. attacking the speaker's idea, evading the speaker, and uniting your ideas together to solve a problem.
   b. uniting your effort, being open, and instructing the other person to solve the problem.
   c. informing the other person, having an open mind, and uniting your efforts to solve a problem.

Chapter 10 Conflict Management

D Read between the lines

Choose the word/phrase that best connects the meanings of the sentence pair.

1. 1) We need a special permit from the school.
   2) They are very strict about selling food.
      a. but   b. because   c. in addition

2. 1) Tom talks a lot about his ideas.
   2) Kazuko keeps quiet.
      a. similarly   b. in addition   c. but

3. 1) She is open to Tom's ideas.
   2) Tom feels happy about it.
      a. but   b. because   c. therefore

4. 1) Yakitori is popular with many people, young and old.
   2) It is easy to cook.
      a. but   b. therefore   c. in addition

5. 1) They discussed the problem.
   2) They could find a solution to the problem.
      a. that is why   b. in contrast   c. however

E Cloze listening

Fill in the gaps with words/phrases from below. Then, listen to the recording and check your answers.

1. evasion	2. communication styles	3. extra time	4. be avoided
5. destructive	6. joining	7. unite	8. be open

Conflicts caused by misunderstanding are common in intercultural situations. Raider and Coleman say people use five a_____ in a conflict situation. These are: attacking, evading, informing, opening, and uniting (AEIOU).

The first one, attacking, is b_____ in communication. It gives people negative feelings towards each other. The second one, c_____, makes the other person very uneasy and anxious. Informing is better. People give useful information and it makes the other person feel better. In the next one, the opening style, the speakers elaborate on the topic. In the last one, the uniting style, the speakers think about their concerns and the other person. By d_____ their efforts they come up with a satisfying solution.

In any conflict situation, we need to take e_____ to inform the other person, f_____ to new ideas, and g_____ our ideas and the other person's. Conflicts caused by misinterpretation and misunderstanding can h_____ by using the IOU type of communication.

Chapter 10 *Conflict Management*

ICC Activity

A What would you do in the following conflict situations? Choose a or b.

1) You and your classmate want to use the computer, but there is only one available.
    a. I will give up using it.
    b. I will tell my classmate I want to use it first.

2) You and a friend want the same library book at the same time.
    a. I will let my friend take it.
    b. I will ask why my classmate wants to borrow it.

3) After playing tennis, you and your sister have to clean up, but you are very tired.
    a. I will ask my sister to clean up for me.
    b. We will clean up together to finish quickly.

4) You and your classmate have to make a group report, but you don't have time.
    a. I'll ask my classmates to do my part.
    b. I will say, "Let's do it together and finish quickly."

5) You and your classmate want to sharpen your pencils at the same time.
    a. I will let my classmate go first.
    b. I will suggest that one of us sharpen both pencils.

B Which of the following sentences uses attacking, evading, informing, opening, or uniting style? Write A, E, I, O, or U after the sentences.

1) Can you explain that in detail so that I can understand it more clearly?
2) You are not telling the truth. You're just making it up, like always.
3) How can we satisfy your needs and at the same time make my wishes come true?
4) I am really too busy to deal with that problem now.
5) The meeting will be from 3:30 to 5:30 in room 1012.

Chapter 11 Cultural Values

"The core of culture is formed by values." (Hofstede, 1991)
「文化の根幹は価値観によって形成されている」

Warm-up

Think of the following situations and answer according to how you feel about it.

1. Your teacher says something. You don't agree. What will you do/say?

2. You have a big exam next week. When will you start studying?

Key words

Match the words in the left column with their meaning in the right column. This will help you understand the reading passage.

1. punctual (　　)
2. element (　　)
3. distinguished lecturer (　　)
4. apology (　　)
5. humor (　　)
6. uphold (　　)
7. propose (　　)
8. power distance (　　)
9. purpose (　　)
10. individualism (　　)
11. collectivism (　　)

a. 支持する
b. 権威ある講演者
c. 権力格差
d. 個人主義
e. 時間厳守の[で]
f. 謝罪
g. 集団主義
h. 提案する
i. 目的
j. ユーモア
k. 要素

READING

The Japanese are generally considered to be "polite and punctual," while Americans are considered to be "frank and friendly." Why? These elements are the main values of each culture. Japanese culture places importance on politeness and punctuality, while American culture places importance on frankness and friendliness.

Here is an example. In Japan if a teacher starts a formal lecture with a friendly joke, he will turn off the audience. Even the most distinguished lecturer starts with a polite apology. Americans always appreciate humor for lecture openings. This makes the lecturer and audience feel closer and relaxed.

Values upheld by cultures and organizations greatly affect people's communication behavior. In 1980, Hofstede proposed four culture values based on data collected from over fifty countries. Each value affects communication.

The first value tells how people accept power differences between people with different ranks. This is called power distance. In organizations, people with higher rank have more power than those with lower rank. In some countries, this is considered desirable but not in others. Hofstede ranked the countries from 1: people most accepting of power difference, to 53: people least accepting of power difference. Malaysia ranked 1st, Japan 33rd, USA 38th, while Austria, 53rd. People use special language to communicate with a person of higher rank. For example, Japanese use honorific language for this purpose.

The second value describes how much people focus on the individual versus the group. This is called individualism vs. collectivism. USA ranked 1st, Japan 22nd, while Guatemala, 53rd. Higher-ranking countries are individualistic societies; they place importance on the individual person. Lower-ranking countries are collectivistic societies; they place importance on the group. These cultural differences influence the way people talk. In collectivistic cultures, when people introduce themselves, they must state the organization they belong to. In individualistic cultures, people talk freely about themselves, and express personal opinions openly.

At work, which is more important, the result or the process — how you do things? Hofstede calls this dimension: masculinity/femininity. In his survey, Japan ranked 1st, USA 15th, and Sweden last. The data showed Japan to be a highly achievement-oriented country. In business, in a result-oriented society, people talk about how much profit was made, rather than how profit was made. People talk more about quantity than quality. According to Hofstede, in general, women uphold process and quality above result and quantity, men uphold result and quantity above process and quality.

The fourth value is attitude towards risk. In some countries, people try to avoid risk, and in other countries people take risks. Greece ranked 1st, Japan ranked 7th, USA 43rd, and Singapore last. You have heard of *nemawashi*, an important business practice in Japan. Japanese do not like to be surprised by sudden proposals; they consult each other before meetings. People avoid taking a risk of saying something that might cause confusion.

In intercultural communication, it's important to know about other people's values to really understand them.

EXERCISES

A New words

Circle the letter that gives the correct meaning of the underlined words/phrases.

1. When a speaker <u>turns off</u> the listeners,
    a. he makes them feel happy.
    b. he gives them good advice.
    c. he makes them feel disappointed.

2. A <u>distinguished</u> lecturer is
    a. a respected person.
    b. a very popular person.
    c. a very rich person.

3. "Americans <u>appreciate</u> humor during lecture openings" means
    a. Americans like humor at the start of a lecture.
    b. Americans like humor to close the lecture.
    c. Americans like humor in the middle of the lecture.

Chapter 11 Cultural Values

4. "In the U.S., people <u>uphold</u> individualism" means
    a. people believe individualism is not good.
    b. people believe individualism makes people rich.
    c. people believe individualism is for everyone.

5. According to the passage, to <u>take a risk</u> means
    a. to do something without thinking.
    b. to plan to do something.
    c. to do something that is uncertain.

B Read for the main ideas

Choose the answer that best completes the meaning of the sentence.

1. According to the passage, important values for Americans are
    a. politeness and friendliness.
    b. politeness and punctuality.
    c. frankness and friendliness.

2. According to the passage, important values for Japanese are
    a. politeness and friendliness.
    b. politeness and punctuality.
    c. frankness and friendliness.

3. When the lecturer in Japan starts a speech with an apology,
    a. the listeners think the lecturer is polite.
    b. the lecturer and listeners feel friendly.
    c. the lecturer and listeners feel close and relaxed.

4. Power distance means
    a. people with high social rank have more power.
    b. people with high social rank have equal power.
    c. people with high social rank have little power.

5. According to the passage, in a collectivistic society,
    a. the individual person is very important.
    b. the group is very important.
    c. the children are very important.

C Read for details

Choose the answer that best completes the meaning of the sentence.

1. According to the passage, in countries with a high degree of power distance,
    a. people have a special polite language.
    b. the individual person is important.
    c. people talk freely about themselves.

2. According to the passage, in a masculine society,
    a. process is more important than result.
    b. result and process are equally important.
    c. result is more important than process.

3. According to the passage, Japanese have "*nemawashi*" because
    a. people do not like to prepare everything before the meeting.
    b. people do not like to talk about a topic suddenly.
    c. people do not like to talk much during a meeting.

4. Among the four values, Japan's highest score is in
    a. collectivism.
    b. power distance.
    c. masculinity.

5. Japan is an achievement-oriented country means in business
    a. people value how much money they make.
    b. people value how they make money.
    c. people value how they use the money.

D Read between the lines

Choose the word/phrase that best connects the meanings of the sentence pair.

1. 1) Polite and punctual are common stereotypes for Japanese.
    2) Frankness and friendliness are common stereotypes for Americans.
        a. similarly   b. in contrast   c. suddenly

2. 1) Americans are individualistic.
    2) People talk freely about themselves.

Chapter 11 Cultural Values

   a. however b. in contrast c. this means

3. 1) People with high rank have more power.

  2) People have a special language for people with higher rank.

   a. in contrast b. however c. in addition

4. 1) In some countries people avoid taking risks.

  2) In other countries people like to take risks.

   a. consequently b. but c. unfortunately

5. 1) It is important to know the values of other people.

  2) You can understand what they say and how they behave.

   a. so that b. unfortunately c. this means

E Cloze listening

Fill in the gaps with words/phrases from below. Then, listen to the recording and check your answers.

1. avoid risks	2. cultural values	3. frankness	4. politeness
5. individualistic	6. cause	7. group	8. collectivist
9. power distance	10. result-oriented society		

  We often hear Japanese are "polite and punctual" while Americans are "frank and friendly." Japanese culture places importance on a_____ and punctuality, while American culture places importance on b_____ and friendliness. These are called c_____.

5 The first cultural value tells how people accept power differences in a society. This means people with different ranks have more power. This is called d_____. In some countries, this is considered desirable but not in others. The second value tells whether society focuses on the individual or the e_____. Countries that give importance to the individual person are 10 called f_____. Countries that give more importance on the group are called g_____. The third value is about result and process. In business,

in a h_____, people talk about how much profit was made, rather than how profit was made. And people talk more about quantity than quality. The fourth value is risk-taking. In some countries, people try to i_____. In some countries, people take risks. For example, in Japan people have *nemawashi*, an important business practice. Japanese consult each other before meetings. They try to avoid discussions that might j_____ confusion. It is important to know about other people's values to really understand what they say and do.

ICC Activity

Check your level of risk-taking. Choose Yes or No.

1) What is different is interesting.   Yes / No
2) I like to be in new places.   Yes / No
3) I feel bored doing the same thing everyday.   Yes / No
4) I do not worry if I don't finish work on time.   Yes / No
5) I can easily talk with new people I meet.   Yes / No
6) What is different is dangerous.   Yes / No
7) I avoid people who are different from me.   Yes / No

Add your scores: Yes = 2 points / No = 1 point
What your score means:

7–9 points	You tend to avoid risk. You are uncomfortable with new things, new places and new people who are different from you. You want to be sure of what will happen next.
10–14 points	You don't mind taking risks. You are comfortable with new things, new places and new people who are different. You can easily adjust.

Chapter 12 Ethnocentrism

"All nice people like Us, are We ... And everyone else is They." (Beebe and Redmond, 2005)

「私たちは善良だが、あいつらは信用できない」

Warm-up

Answer the following questions.

You meet a foreigner for the first time in Tokyo. What questions would you ask him/her? List in the order you will ask, from first to last.

Q
1. What is your name?
2. Do you study/work in Japan?
3. Do you like Japan/Japanese people?
4. Do you like your school/job?
5. Do you eat raw fish in your country?
6. What sports [kind of music] do you like?
7. How is the weather in your country?
8. Do you often get caught in a crowded train like this?

Key words

Match the words in the left column with their meaning in the right column. This will help you understand the reading passage.

1. inferior to (　　)   a. 遅れた文化
2. superior to (　　)   b. 駆け足で通って
3. be intrigued by (　　)   c. 直接会う
4. mount on (horseback) (　　)   d. 文化の中の未知の部分
5. galloping through (　　)   e. 〜に魅せられる
6. backward culture (　　)   f. 〜に基づいて
7. wait in line (　　)   g. （馬に）またがる
8. according to (　　)   h. 〜より劣る
9. meet firsthand (　　)   i. 〜より優る
10. unfamiliar elements of culture (　　)   j. 列について待つ

READING

Oftentimes, we feel strange when we see people from other countries doing things differently from the way we do them. We feel those people are unusual and backward compared to us. This feeling is called ethnocentrism. It is a negative attitude towards other things and other people because you believe your culture is the best. This word also means judging other cultures as inferior to your own.

It is important to be proud of one's culture and lifestyle. When this pride is too strong, we tend to view our group as the center of everything. We think of it as superior to all others. When we see other groups, we compare them with ours, and we finally judge them as inferior.

Marilyn's experience in Russia is an example. Marilyn had always been intrigued by Russia, and had always dreamed of traveling to the country. She wanted to explore Moscow, St. Petersburg and other places in the country. Her first day of the trip was a disappointing experience, though. When she arrived in Moscow, she joined a village tour where she saw a very different wedding ceremony. She was shocked to see women in gowns mounted on horseback and galloping through the park. The men, half-drunk, were cheering amidst fireworks, and were dancing wildly to a brass band. Marilyn sniffed, "What kind of people are these?" The tourist guide said, "This is our custom here." Marilyn remarked, "But that's very wild. I've never seen anything like that. What a backward culture."

Obviously, Marilyn made this judgment because she had been used to formal wedding celebrations in a very formal manner.

Keiko's experience is another example. Keiko came back from a trip to China. Almost crying, she said, "I will never go there again." When the teacher asked why, Keiko said, "I was there for four days; no one waited in line. Chinese are so rude." The teacher asked, "Have you been to all of China?" The student said, "I only went to one city."

Keiko was expecting all Chinese people to behave like Japanese who wait in line. Because some Chinese did not, she judged all Chinese according to her cultural standard.

To avoid this negative attitude, there are some things we need to do. First, we need to gain more correct knowledge of different groups of people and their lifestyle. More knowledge does not mean only acquiring more information. Greater positive contact with other people is also essential. Culture contact is possible by traveling and meeting firsthand with people we do not really know about. By increasing personal relationships, usually by making friends with people from a different cultural background, we develop positive feelings about them. We need to learn at least a little of the language of another culture. By learning and speaking the language of another place, we begin to understand the unfamiliar elements of the culture and gain more of an appreciation of the people and the place. Appreciation comes from better understanding.

When you see children swimming in a dirty river, when you see people eating with their fingers, how do you feel?

EXERCISES

A New words

Circle the letter that gives the correct meaning of the underlined words/phrases.

1. According to the passage, <u>ethnocentrism</u> is
    a. a negative feeling that arises when we see other people who are not from our own culture.
    b. a positive feeling when we see other people from our own culture.
    c. an expression that is the same for people in most cultures.

2. When we judge another culture as <u>inferior</u>,
    a. we think our group is the best.
    b. we think our culture is the same as others.
    c. we think other cultures are better.

3. When we are <u>proud of</u> our culture,
    a. we think our group is the center of everything.
    b. we think other cultures are better than ours.
    c. we compare our culture with others.

4. Marilyn said "the village had a backward culture" because
    a. the men and women in the village were celebrating.
    b. she did not like the men and women in the village.
    c. the men and women in the village acted strangely to her.

5. According to the passage, "appreciation comes from better understanding" means
    a. we come to understand another culture better when we like it.
    b. we come to like another culture better when we know more about it.
    c. we come to like another culture better when we speak the language.

B Read for the main ideas

Choose the answer that best completes the meaning of the sentence.

1. Ethnocentrism is not a good feeling or attitude because
    a. we tend to believe other cultures are better than ours.
    b. we feel strange.
    c. we believe our culture is the best and judge others as inferior.

2. Marilyn traveled to Moscow because
    a. she had always been interested in Russia.
    b. she wanted to go to the wedding ceremony.
    c. she wanted to join a tour group.

3. Marilyn was shocked when she saw the wedding ceremony because
    a. it was very noisy.
    b. it was very different from what she had seen before.
    c. the horses and the men were drunk.

4. Keiko did not want to go to China again because
    a. the people she met were always in line.
    b. the people she met were always on time.
    c. the people she met did not wait in line.

5. When we know and speak the language of another culture
    a. we appreciate the people and the place better.
    b. we can understand our culture better.
    c. we can understand our feelings better.

Chapter 12 Ethnocentrism

C Read for details

Choose the answer that best completes the meaning of the sentence.

1. According to the passage, when we see people from other cultures do things differently,
   a. we become proud of our own culture.
   b. we think they are strange.
   c. we gain appreciation for them.

2. According to the passage, when we think our culture is the best
   a. we can understand other people better.
   b. we judge other cultures as superior.
   c. we judge other cultures as inferior.

3. Marilyn's first day in Moscow was a disappointing experience because
   a. she saw a strange kind of wedding ceremony.
   b. the women were galloping with the horse.
   c. the tourist guide was not helpful.

4. Culture contact is possible by
   a. studying a foreign language that we do not know.
   b. being proud of our culture and comparing it with others.
   c. traveling and meeting firsthand with people we do not really know about.

5. According to the passage, which of the following is NOT true?
   a. We need to gain more correct knowledge of other people and their lifestyles.
   b. Little knowledge helps us understand people more.
   c. Greater positive contact with other people is essential.

D Read between the lines

Choose the word/phrase that best connects the meanings of the sentence pair.

1. 1) Ethnocentrism is a negative attitude towards other things and other people.
   2) It means judging other cultures as inferior to your own.
      a. therefore   b. similarly   c. in other words

87

2. 1) It is important to be proud of one's culture and lifestyle.
   2) When this pride becomes too strong, we think we are the center of everything.
      a. consequently   b. but   c. as a result

3. 1) Keiko was shocked at the behavior of some Chinese people.
   2) She was expecting them to behave like Japanese.
      a. because   b. in contrast   c. similarly

4. 1) Marilyn was surprised to see an unfamiliar type of wedding ceremony in Moscow.
   2) Keiko was surprised to see Chinese behave differently from Japanese.
      a. in contrast   b. similarly   c. therefore

5. 1) When you speak the language of the country, you will understand the people better.
   2) You will appreciate the culture and its lifestyle more.
      a. in contrast   b. otherwise   c. therefore

E Cloze listening

Fill in the gaps with words/phrases from below. Then, listen to the recording and check your answers.

1. making friends   2. inferior to   3. and backward
4. negative attitude   5. our understanding   6. we appreciate
7. too strong   8. judge them   9. positive contact   10. by traveling

    Oftentimes, we feel strange when we see people from other countries do things differently. We feel those people are unusual a_____ compared to us. This feeling is called ethnocentrism. It is a b_____ towards other things and other people because you believe your culture is the best. The word ethnocentrism also means judging other cultures as c_____ your own.

    It is important to be proud of one's culture and lifestyle. But when this pride is

88

Chapter 12 Ethnocentrism

d_____, we tend to view our group as the center of everything. We think of it as superior to all others. When we see other groups, we compare them with ours, and we finally e_____ as inferior.

To avoid this negative attitude, there are some things we need to do. First, we need to increase f_____ of different groups of people and their lifestyles. Increased knowledge does not mean only increased information. Greater g_____ with other people is also essential. Direct contact with people and a new place is also called culture contact. Culture contact is possible h_____ and meeting firsthand with people we do not really know well. When we increase personal relationship, usually by i_____ with people from a different cultural background, we develop positive feelings about them. We also need to know the language of another culture. By knowing and speaking the language of another place, we begin to understand all the unfamiliar elements of that culture. Finally, j_____ the people and the place better. Appreciation comes from greater understanding.

ICC Activity

Check your ethnocentrism scale.

A Circle the number 5 (strongly agree), 4 (agree), 3 (neutral), 2 (disagree), or 1 (strongly disagree) according to how you feel or think about each of the statements.

1) Most cultures are backward compared to (Japan) my culture.

   5   4   3   2   1

2) My culture (Japan) should be the model for other cultures.

   5   4   3   2   1

3) Lifestyles in other cultures are just as good as in (Japan) my culture.*

   5   4   3   2   1

4) People from my culture (Japanese) can learn a lot from other people.*

   5   4   3   2   1

5) The lifestyle in my culture (Japan) is the best and most comfortable.

   5   4   3   2   1

6) I do not trust people who are different.

   5   4   3   2   1

B Which of the following pairs would you choose? You might like both but you must make a choice.

1) a. a shower   b. a bathtub
2) a. corn soup   b. miso soup
3) a. hamburger   b. sushi
4) a. sit on a sofa   b. sit on the tatami mat
5) a. spaghetti   b. soba (Japanese noodles)

Chapter 13 Barriers to Communication: Stereotypes

"First impressions always last; but they can be wrong. We should always move beyond first impressions quickly." (Campbell, 2005)

「第一印象は記憶に残るが、必ずしも正確ではない。第一印象に留まるのではなく、人間関係を前進させよう」

Warm-up

Look at the picture and answer the questions that follow.

Q
1. What do you think is the woman's occupation? Why?
2. What do you think her nationality is? Why do you think so?
3. Where do you think she came from? What made you say that?
4. Where do you think she is going? Why do you think so?

Key words

Match the words in the left column with their meaning in the right column. This will help you understand the reading passage.

1. blonde hair (　　)
2. a fair complexion (　　)
3. a rigid image (　　)
4. an inflexible idea (　　)
5. inaccurate (　　)
6. interpret ~ behavior (　　)
7. liar (　　)
8. a skin allergy (　　)
9. generalize (　　)
10. anthropologist (　　)

a. 一般化する
b. 色白
c. うそつき
d. 堅苦しいイメージ
e. 金髪
f. 柔軟性のない考え方
g. 人類学者
h. ～の行動（行為）を解釈する
i. 皮膚のアレルギー
j. 不正確な

READING

A stereotype is a set of images that we have about a person, a thing or a group of people. Stereotypes are very common everywhere, and in our daily life. In the picture in the previous page, some students immediately think the lady is an American because she has blonde hair, blue eyes and a fair complexion. This is a stereotype of Americans. Some students think she is a businesswoman because of her clothes, or because she is carrying a briefcase. A common stereotype of businessmen or businesswomen is wearing a suit and carrying a briefcase.

Usually, these rigid images or inflexible ideas are inaccurate or not true. When we stereotype people, we put them in a box, or a category, and we interpret their behavior based on images we have. We always hear "Americans are friendly, individualistic, talkative and noisy. They talk more about themselves than about others." "Japanese are the opposite. They are group-oriented, shy and hardworking." "Chinese are business-minded." "Asian students are good at math." These are examples of international stereotypes.

Where do our stereotypes come from? We usually develop images of people, places and things from our own personal experience. Sho, a Japanese student, went to study in the U.S. Every day, from his apartment, he would see students playing baseball from morning until night. When Sho came back to Japan, he was so excited to tell his friends, "American students are very good baseball players." His image of American students was formed by what he saw every day during his stay in the U.S.

Sometimes our images of people are formed by stories we hear. One housewife remarked angrily: "I don't believe salesmen anymore; they are liars." When I asked her why, she said: "My sister got a skin allergy after using the face lotion a saleslady recommended to her." This woman has a negative impression of all salespeople because of her sister's experience.

Most of the time, stereotypes come from the mass media, for example "All Europeans dress fashionably." Some foreigners come to Japan for the first time with the expectation that "Japanese are polite and hardworking."

Because stereotypes are usually inaccurate images, they make us simplify or generalize people that we meet. Stereotypes can become a barrier to effective intercultural communication. They prevent us from seeing the uniqueness of something, or of an individual, or a group of people. During your first meeting with someone from another culture, you react toward him based on your stereotypes about the stranger's culture. Interestingly, when an American and a Japanese businessman meet for the first time, typically the American bows, while the Japanese extends his hand to shake hands. We also learn stereotypes as part of our culture. Two anthropologists suggest that "every person is, in some ways, like all other people, like some people, and like no other people." When we meet other people, the challenge is to see how they are alike, and how they are unique. Before that, we have to check our own stereotypes.

EXERCISES

A New words

Circle the letter that gives the correct meaning of the underlined words/phrases.

1. A common <u>stereotype</u> of a businessman means
   a. people's fixed image of a businessman.
   b. people's feelings toward a businessman.
   c. people's natural behavior toward a businessman.

2. We develop <u>rigid images</u> of a person when
   a. we write about that person.
   b. baseball players tell us about that person.
   c. we hear and experience about that person.

3. Our <u>inflexible</u> ideas about someone or something
   a. are usually correct.
   b. are usually not clear.
   c. are usually not true.

4. When you are <u>individualistic</u>, you
   a. are friendly.
   b. are noisy.
   c. think of yourself more than others.

5. According to the passage, a <u>liar</u> is
    a. a person who tells the truth.
    b. a person who does not tell the truth.
    c. a person who sells face lotion.

B Read for the main ideas

Choose the answer that best completes the meaning of the sentence.

1. The most common stereotype of Americans is
    a. friendly, noisy and group-oriented.
    b. polite, shy and group-oriented.
    c. friendly, noisy and individualistic.

2. The passage explains
    a. two possible ways we form stereotypes.
    b. three possible ways we form stereotypes.
    c. four possible ways we form stereotypes.

3. An example of an international stereotype is
    a. Europeans are fashionable.
    b. Sho studied in the U.S.
    c. businessmen wear suits and carry a suitcase.

4. Stereotypes are bad because
    a. they help us read the mass media.
    b. they prevent us from seeing the uniqueness of a person.
    c. they help us meet people for the first time.

5. Stereotypes do not give us correct views of other people because
    a. we generalize everybody's experience.
    b. we simplify communication.
    c. we oversimplify or make generalizations about things and people.

C Read for details

Choose the answer that best completes the meaning of the sentence.

Chapter 13 Barriers to Communication: Stereotypes

1. Most people from other countries think that Japanese are
    a. friendly, polite and individualistic.
    b. talkative, friendly and individualistic.
    c. polite, shy and group-oriented.

2. Students think the woman in the picture is an American because
    a. she is wearing a suit.
    b. she has blonde hair, blue eyes and a fair complexion.
    c. she is carrying a briefcase.

3. Sho thinks all American students are good at baseball because
    a. he played baseball with them every day.
    b. he told them to play baseball every day.
    c. he saw some American students play baseball every day.

4. The housewife has a bad impression of all salespeople because
    a. her sister lied about the face lotion.
    b. the saleslady sold her sister some bad face lotion.
    c. the saleslady charged her too much for some face lotion.

5. When we meet someone for the first time, we should
    a. see how unique he/she is.
    b. face his/her problem.
    c. challenge him/her.

D Read between the lines

Choose the word/phrase that best connects the meanings of the sentence pair.

1. 1) Students think she is a businessperson.
   2) She was wearing suits and carrying a suitcase.
       a. because   b. suddenly   c. actually

2. 1) When we stereotype people, we put them in a box.
   2) We have a rigid image about them and interpret their behavior accordingly.
       a. similarly   b. in other words   c. however

3. 1) Americans are friendly, talkative and individualistic.
   2) Japanese are shy, quiet and group-oriented.

a. actually   b. because   c. in contrast

4. 1) We have stereotypes from our personal experiences.
   2) We have stereotypes from other people's experiences.
   a. in contrast   b. in addition   c. in other words

5. 1) Stereotyping is a barrier to intercultural communication.
   2) It prevents us from seeing the uniqueness of the people we meet.
   a. because   b. however   c. in contrast

E Cloze listening

Fill in the gaps with words/phrases from below. Then, listen to the recording and check your answers.

1. not true	2. hard working	3. the mass media
4. a box	5. about themselves	6. good at
7. simplify	8. experiences	9. a barrier	10. uniqueness

Stereotypes are images we have about a person or a group of people, places or things. Usually, these rigid images or impressions are inaccurate or a_____. When we stereotype people, we put them in b_____ and we interpret their behavior based on images we have. We often hear that "Americans are friendly, individualistic, talkative and noisy." They talk more c_____ than others. "Japanese are the opposite," is another stereotype. "They are group-oriented, shy and d_____." "Chinese are business minded." "Asian students are e_____ math." These are examples of international stereotypes.

Where do stereotypes come from? We usually develop images of people, places and things from our own f_____. Sometimes we form images of people from stories we hear. Most of the time, our stereotypes come from what we see and what we hear from g_____.

Because stereotypes are inaccurate images they make us h_____ or

Chapter 13 Barriers to Communication: Stereotypes

15 make generalizations about people that we meet. Stereotypes can become i_____ to effective intercultural communication. They prevent us from seeing the j_____ of something, an individual, or a group of people.

ICC Activity

1. Write down images that come to your mind when you hear the following words.

    1) Cowboy

    ---

    2) Scientist

    ---

    3) Salesman

    ---

    4) Chinese

    ---

    5) England

    ---

    6) Youth

    ---

2. Compare your images with a classmate. Discuss the following.

    1) What are the common images you and your classmates have?
    2) How did you get those images?
    3) Are those images (stereotypes) good or bad?

Chapter 14 Barriers to Communication: Prejudice

"We cannot totally get rid of prejudice altogether. But we can do something by being aware of it." (Rogers and Steinfatt, 1999)

「私たちは偏見をすべてなくすことはできないかもしれないが、偏見に気づくことで、偏見に基づいた行動をとらないようにすることはできる」(Rogers and Steinfatt, 1999)

Warm-up

Look at the pictures and answer the questions that follow.

A   B

Q
1. How would you feel in the following situations?
   A: A friend (foreigner) gives you food from his/her plate. Smiling, he/she says, "try this; it's good."
   B: Everyone around you eats with their fingers. You must do the same.

2. Why did you feel that way in those situations?

Key words

Match the words on the left column with their meaning on the right column. They will help you understand the reading passage.

1. ignore (　　)   a. 裁判に訴える
2. deceive (　　)   b. だます
3. go to court (　　)   c. 〜に基づいて行動する
4. ask ~ directions (　　)   d. （コミュニケーション）の壁
5. prior to (　　)   e. 〜の前に
6. act on (　　)   f. 文化的原因による盲目
7. violent (　　)   g. 暴力的な
8. a barrier to (communication) (　　) h. 〜に道順をたずねる
9. cultural blindness (　　)   i. 無視する

Chapter 14 Barriers to Communication: Prejudice

READING

Prejudice is a negative attitude towards another person or group of people based on a comparison with your own group. The word "prejudice" comes from two root words:
5 pre and judge. This means judging another person or group before you actually come in contact with them. This feeling is usually a result of negative or false stereotype.

Here is an example. One day in school, a
10 student said that she met an "African" man in the hallway who was asking her questions in English. The young woman ran away and ignored him. In her next class, she told the teacher her story. When the teacher asked why she did not help him, she said she was afraid because of his height and color, and she was afraid he would deceive her. The
15 teacher explained that the man was a guest lecturer who had given a presentation at the university the day before; he just came back to get something in the classroom. He just wanted to ask the young woman directions to the classroom.

Here is another example. A group of foreigners in Japan went to court because they were not allowed to enter a hot spring. During the investigation, it was found that
20 prior to this incident, some foreign visitors coming to the hot spring did not follow the rules and made the place dirty. The owner got so mad that he decided not to allow foreigners to enter the hot spring anymore.

Prejudice comes in many forms. The examples above show that sometimes people act based on their negative feelings. The young woman ran away from the African lecturer.
25 The Japanese hot spring owner banned the foreigners from the hot spring. When people act on their negative feelings, they discriminate against people. Prejudice leads to discrimination, which is the topic of the next chapter.

There are other types of prejudice. Some prejudices are not manifested. We cannot see them and therefore we cannot act on them. Because prejudice is an emotion, they
30 stay in people's hearts. For example, many prejudiced North Americans have a negative stereotype of African Americans. They perceive African Americans as poor, lazy, and violent, among other culture groups in the U.S.

As you can see, prejudice is a strong negative feeling or attitude that may be caused by stories we hear from other people, something we heard from the mass media, or probably our own unpleasant experience. Prejudice is a barrier to communication; it prevents us from interacting with new people and seeing reality accurately. Prejudice is a kind of cultural blindness.

How can we deal with prejudice? Can we avoid it? The first thing you have to do is be aware of your prejudice. Everyone has prejudice against something or someone. Being aware of your own prejudices leads to the next step: do not act on your prejudice. Finally, it is important to get a lot of accurate information. By knowing about differences between people, you will be able to understand them and get rid of negative feelings.

EXERCISES

A New words

Circle the letter that gives the correct meaning of the underlined words/phrases.

1. According to the passage, <u>prejudice</u> means
    a. to judge a person or a group before you actually meet him/them.
    b. to judge a person or a group when you actually meet him/them.
    c. to judge a person or a group after you actually meet him/them.

2. "The young woman <u>ignored the man</u>" also means
    a. she answered his questions.
    b. she helped him find the room.
    c. she ran away.

3. When the foreigners <u>went to court</u>, they
    a. asked the judge to check on the problem.
    b. asked the hot spring owner to check on the problem.
    c. asked other foreigners to come to the hot spring.

4. When some prejudices are <u>not manifested</u>, they
    a. can be seen.
    b. can be solved.
    c. stay in people's hearts.

5. Prejudice is a <u>barrier to</u> communication because
   a. it helps us see people accurately.
   b. it prevents us from seeing people accurately.
   c. it tells us to see people accurately.

B Read for the main ideas

Choose the answer that best completes the meaning of the sentence.

1. According to the passage, people usually have a negative feeling for others
   a. because of a false or negative stereotype.
   b. because of friends.
   c. because of too much fear.

2. The young woman ran away from the man because
   a. she was afraid of him.
   b. he deceived her.
   c. the teacher told her to run away.

3. The owner did not allow the foreigners into the hot spring because
   a. they made the hot spring dirty.
   b. other foreigners made the hot spring dirty.
   c. the hot spring was dirty.

4. The passage is trying to say that to be able to communicate with people,
   a. we must be friendly.
   b. we must avoid saying bad things.
   c. we must avoid having negative feelings.

5. The passage gives _____ to overcome prejudice.
   a. one suggestion
   b. two suggestions
   c. three suggestions

C Read for details

Choose the answer that best completes the meaning of the sentence.

1. The African lecturer returned to the university
   a. because he wanted to chat with the students.
   b. because he wanted to talk with the teacher.
   c. because he wanted to get something he forgot.

2. Some North Americans have a negative stereotype of African Americans because
   a. they think African Americans are poor, lazy and violent.
   b. African Americans are poor, lazy and violent.
   c. the media says African Americas are poor, lazy and violent.

3. Prejudice is also a kind of cultural blindness because
   a. it prevents us from seeing other people accurately.
   b. it helps us see other people accurately.
   c. it encourages us to see other people accurately.

4. Which of the following statements is NOT true?
   a. Everyone has prejudice against something or someone.
   b. You should be aware of your prejudice.
   c. It is impossible to deal with foreigners.

5. When prejudice can be seen, it can be solved, but when prejudice cannot be seen,
   a. it stays in people's hearts.
   b. we cannot do anything about it.
   c. it comes from an unpleasant experience.

D Read between the lines

Choose the word/phrase that best connects the meanings of the sentence pair.

1. 1) The African man came back to get something he forgot in the classroom.
   2) He just wanted to ask her directions to the classroom.
      a. suddenly   b. surprisingly   c. actually

Chapter 14 Barriers to Communication: Prejudice

2. 1) Some foreigners came to the hot spring but did not follow the rules of the place.
   2) The owner got so mad that he decided not to allow foreigners to enter anymore.
       a. therefore   b. however   c. suddenly

3. 1) Many prejudiced North Americans have a negative image of African Americans.
   2) They perceive African Americans as poor, lazy, and violent.
       a. for example   b. on the other hand   c. interestingly

4. 1) Some unpleasant situations create problems which people can solve.
   2) When people act on their negative feelings, they discriminate against people.
       a. fortunately   b. however   c. suddenly

5. 1) Can we avoid prejudice?
   2) You need to be aware of your prejudices.
       a. for example   b. first of all   c. however

E Cloze listening

Fill in the gaps with words/phrases from below. Then, listen to the recording and check your answers.

1. act on	2. based on	3. in contact	4. prevents us
5. not manifested	6. interacting with	7. create problems	
8. deal with	9. correct information	10. the mass media	

    Prejudice is a negative attitude towards another person or group of people a_____ a comparison with your group. This means judging another person or group negatively before you actually come b_____ with them.
    Prejudice comes in many forms. The first type is a negative feeling that leads to unpleasant situations that c_____, like discrimination. Another type of prejudice is d_____. We can't see it, and therefore we can't

103

e_____ it. Because prejudice is an emotion, it stays in people's hearts.
   This strong negative feeling or attitude is usually caused by stories we hear based on another person's experience, something we heard from f_____, or probably our own unpleasant experience. Prejudice is a barrier to communication; it g_____ from seeing reality accurately and h_____ new people. Prejudice is a kind of cultural blindness.
   How can we i_____ prejudice? First, be aware of your own prejudice. Being aware of your prejudice leads to the next step. Next, do not act on your prejudice. Finally, it is important to get a lot of j_____. By knowing about differences between people, you will be able to understand them and get rid of negative feelings.

ICC Activity

Choose a partner and discuss the following.

1. What would you do in the following situations?

    1) You and your friend are sitting and eating lunch in the park. An old man in dirty clothes approaches you and asks you something. What will you do?
        a. I will listen.
        b. I will run away.
        c. I will pretend I didn't understand him. Why?

    2) You are on a platform in Tokyo waiting for a train. A foreigner approaches you asking for something. What will you do?
        a. I will listen.
        b. I will run away.
        c. I will pretend I didn't understand him. Why?

2. Compare your images with a classmate.

Chapter 15 Barriers to Communication: Discrimination

"All of us are in a symphony. We each play a different tune, but we all make the same music." (Beebe and Redmond, 2005)

「私たちは交響楽団の一員のようなものだ。それぞれ異なる旋律を演奏するが、みんな同じ曲を演奏している」

Warm-up

Look at the following signs. What do you feel when you see them?

Sign 1

Sign 2

Key words

Match the words in the left column with their meaning in the right column. This will help you understand the reading passage.

1. unfair treatment （　　）
2. reject （　　）
3. ethnicity （　　）
4. racism （　　）
5. hierarchy (among races) （　　）
6. be denied （　　）
7. be punished （　　）
8. gender discrimination （　　）
9. pass (a law) （　　）

a. （人種間の）上下関係
b. 人種差別
c. 性差別
d. （法律を）成立させる
e. 罰せられる
f. 否定される
g. 不公平な扱い
h. 民族性
i. 拒否する

READING

When a negative feeling or attitude like a prejudice, which we studied in Chapter 14, leads to an action, the result is discrimination. Action based on prejudice results in unfair treatment of people. Examples include rejecting or treating an individual or group of people unfairly because of their age, gender, ethnicity, or physical attributes such as skin and hair color, or facial structure.

There are many different types of discrimination. The most common type is called racial discrimination. Racial discrimination is usually a result of racism, a belief that there is a hierarchy among human races, and that your race is the best. Racism is a strong form of ethnocentrism. Many years ago in the United States, African-American children were not allowed to attend the same schools as white children. Many whites believed that blacks were stupid, lazy, and violent, and there were strong fears that black children would cause trouble in school. As a result, these children were denied the right to a good education, which was obviously a form of discrimination against black children.

In Chapter 14, we learned that the hot spring owner was very angry with some foreigners who made the place dirty. Because of this experience, he developed a strong negative feeling against foreigners. When his feelings turned into action — not allowing foreigners into the hot spring — he discriminated against them. He was punished because of what he did. No one can punish you because you are angry. But once you do something because of your anger, you can be punished for your action, like the hot spring owner.

Another type of discrimination is gender discrimination. In the past, women were not given the opportunity to work outside the home. Even when women were allowed to work outside the home, they received less pay. People thought they couldn't perform as well as men. In 1979, the U.N. adopted an agreement to end discrimination against women in all forms. Most countries have ratified the idea into law.

Another form of discrimination is age discrimination. In the past, older people were denied jobs, were dismissed from work, or were not paid or not treated equally. In the U.S., a new law was made (effective from Oct. 2006) to make sure that older people, especially those 40 years or older, could have equal opportunities for pay, training and promotion.

Like stereotypes and prejudice, discrimination is obviously a barrier to intercultural

Chapter 15 Barriers to Communication: Discrimination

communication. It prevents you from building positive relationships with other people.

How does discrimination develop? As mentioned in Chapter 14, when people allow their negative feelings against others to get out of control, they tend to act on their feelings. White people had fears about black children, so they discriminated against them. How can we prevent discrimination? There are some things you can do. First, be aware of your negative feelings. By knowing your emotions, you can check, control and re-direct them. Also, there must be a shift — a change of attitude and behavior.

EXERCISES

A New words

Circle the letter that gives the correct meaning of the underlined words/phrases.

1. According to the passage, <u>discrimination</u> means
    a. a negative feeling against a person or group.
    b. a negative attitude against a person or group.
    c. an action that comes when you have a negative feeling against someone.

2. <u>Racism</u> means
    a. you think people who look like you are the best.
    b. you think that men are better than women.
    c. you think children cause trouble in school.

3. According to the passage, you can be <u>punished</u>
    a. when you get angry.
    b. when you discriminate.
    c. when you treat someone nicely.

4. Women can enjoy <u>equal treatment</u> with men means
    a. women can work and get higher pay than men do.

107

　　　　b. women can work and get lower pay than men do.

　　　　c. women can work and get the same pay as men do.

5. There is <u>a shift</u> in your attitude when
　　　　a. you keep your attitude the same.
　　　　b. you change your attitude.
　　　　c. you talk about your attitude.

B Read for the main ideas

Choose the answer that best completes the meaning of the sentence.

1. According to the passage, discrimination
　　　　a. is a result of prejudice.
　　　　b. is a result of stereotypes.
　　　　c. is a result of human races.

2. The most common type of discrimination is
　　　　a. facial discrimination.
　　　　b. racial discrimination.
　　　　c. gender discrimination.

3. The hot spring owner was punished because
　　　　a. the foreigners made the place dirty.
　　　　b. he did not pay the foreigners.
　　　　c. he did not allow the foreigners to enter the hot spring.

4. After the law was passed in 1979,
　　　　a. women could enjoy the same jobs and pay as men.
　　　　b. women could discriminate against men.
　　　　c. women could work more than men.

5. The passage talks about
　　　　a. four types of discrimination.
　　　　b. three types of discrimination.
　　　　c. two types of discrimination.

Chapter 15 Barriers to Communication: Discrimination

C Read for details

Choose the answer that best completes the meaning of the sentence.

1. According to the passage, discrimination results in
   a. an action based on fairness.
   b. unfair treatment of people.
   c. the belief that your country is the best.

2. African-American children were not allowed to go to the same schools as white children because
   a. people feared they would make the school dirty.
   b. people feared they would get low grades.
   c. people feared they would cause trouble.

3. The hot spring owner did not allow the foreigners to go inside because
   a. the foreigners did not pay.
   b. he had negative feelings against foreigners.
   c. the foreigners went to court.

4. Not allowing black children to go to the same schools as white children is
   a. a form of justice.
   b. an example of racial discrimination.
   c. an example of gender discrimination.

5. The law of 1979 is important because
   a. it ended all types of discrimination.
   b. it ended all types of racial discrimination.
   c. it ended all types of gender discrimination.

D Read between the lines

Choose the word/phrase that best connects the meanings of the sentence pair.

1. 1) Discrimination is an action based on prejudice.
   2) It includes treating someone unfairly because of his race, skin color, etc.
      a. suddenly   b. surprisingly   c. in addition

2. 1) Racial discrimination is the most common type of discrimination.

109

2) Children of African Americans could not go to the same schools as white children.

    a. in contrast   b. for example   c. however

3. 1) One foreigner customer made the hot spring spa dirty.
   2) The owner developed strong negative feelings against all foreigners.

    a. as a result   b. similarly   c. in addition

4. 1) Ethnocentrism means "My people are the best."
   2) Racism means "All other people are not good."

    a. suddenly   b. in contrast   c. finally

5. 1) Women could not enjoy equal treatment.
   2) People believed men could perform better than woman in the workplace.

    a. similarly   b. in contrast   c. because

E Cloze listening

Fill in the gaps with words/phrases from below. Then, listen to the recording and check your answers.

1. feared them	2. human races	3. most common
4. physical qualities	5. rejecting	6. fewer cases
7. unequal treatment	8. racism	9. the best	10. owner

Discrimination is an action which is the result of a negative feeling against someone or a group of people. The a_____ action includes b_____ or treating someone unfairly because of age, gender, race, and c_____ such as skin and hair color, or facial structure.

5   Racial discrimination comes from d_____, a belief that there is a hierarchy of e_____, and your country and your race is f_____. Black children were discriminated against because white people g_____. Foreigners were discriminated because the Japanese hot spring h_____ did not like them. Gender discrimination, or i_____

Chapter 15 Barriers to Communication: Discrimination

10 of women, happened because people believed that men could perform better than women in the workplace. Fortunately today, there are j_____ of discrimination. Have you ever been discriminated against by someone?

ICC Activity

A Make groups of 4 or 5. Choose one topic below, discuss and give examples. You can do it in English or Japanese.

1) age discrimination
2) gender discrimination
3) ethnic discrimination
4) physical discrimination

Report to the class after discussion.

B Have you ever felt you have been discriminated against? Where? When? Why? How? Share your experience.

C Look at the following expressions. Do you feel anything when you hear them?

1) Go back home, white men!
2) We don't accept yellow monkeys here.
3) "You're Japanese? You don't need a visa to enter the U.S.! "
   "You're from Thailand? Then, you must get a visa to enter the U.S."

111

References

Chapter 1
1. Ekman, et al (1972) In Donald Klopf & Satoshi Ishii *Communicating without words* (Tokyo: NanUndo, 1987). p. 27.
2. Levine, Deena & Adelman, Mara. *Beyond Language.* (New York: Prentice Hall, 1993)
3. Klopf, Donald and Ishii, Satoshi, op. cit.
4. Levine D. and Adelman, M. op cit.

Chapter 2
1. Levine D. and Adelman, M. op cit. p.104.
2. Ibid, p. 104.
3. Klopf Donald and Ishii, Satoshi op cit. p. 15.

Chapter 3
1. Hall, Edward. *The Hidden Dimension.* (New York, Doubleday. 1966) pp. 126-127.
2. Adapted from Levine & Adelman, op cit. pp. 108-110.
3. Collett, P. "Training Englishmen in the non-verbal behavior of Arabs," *International Journal of Psychology* 6 (1971), pp.209-215.

Chapter 4
1. Hall, Edward. *The Silent Language.* (New York: Doubleday, 1959).
2. Rogers, Everett & Steinfatt, Thomas. *Intercultural Communication.* (Illinois: Waveland Press, 1999) p. 181.
3. Hall, E. op cit.
4. Adapted from Klopf and Ishii, Time and Culture in *Communicating without Words,* op cit. pp. 80-90.
5. Rich, W. (1989). *International Handbook of Corporate Communication.* Jefferson, NC: McFarland. (In Africa where a slow pace is valued, people who rush are suspected of trying to cheat.)
6. Morrison, Terri and Connaway, Wayne. *Kiss, Bow or Shake Hands.* (Adams Media Corporation, 2006).

Chapter 5
1. Tannen, Deborah. *You Just Don't Understand: Women and men in conversation.* (Ballantine Books: NY, 1990)
2. Ibid, p. 74
3. Ibid, p. 123

Chapter 6
1. Donaue, Ray. *Japanese culture language and communication.* (University Press of America: Maryland, 1998).
2. Sakamoto, Nancy and Naotso, Reiko. *Polite Fictions: Why Japanese and Americans Seem Rude* (Tokyo: Kinseido Ltd., 1982), p. 81.
3. Donaue, R. op. cit.
4. Tannen, D. op. cit. pp. 195-202.

Chapter 7
Barnlund, Dean. *Public and private self in Japan and the United States.* (Tokyo, Japan: The Simul Press, 1975).

Chapter 8
1. Bower, Sharon and Bower, Gordon. *Asserting Your-Self.* (Perseus Books. 1991) pp.87-105
2. Hartley, Peter. *Interpersonal Communication.* (Rutledge: London, 1999). pp.193-195.

Chapter 9
1. Donahue, R. op. cit. pp. 147-149.
2. Hartley, P. op. cit. pp. 58-59.
3. Cornelious, Helena, Faire, Shoshana, and Cornelius, Estella *Everyone Can Win*. (Sydney, Simon & Schuster, 1989) pp. 37-55.

Chapter 10
1. Raider, Ellen; Coleman, Susan and Gerson, Janet. "Teaching Conflict Resolution Skills in a Workshop." In Morton Deutsch and Peter Coleman(Eds.), *The Handbook of Conflict Resolution*. (Jossey-Bass, 2000) pp.499-521.

Chapter 11
1. Adapted from Susan Beebe, Steven Beebe and Mark Redmond, *Interpersonal Communication* (NY: Pearson Education, 2005), p. 99.
2. Everett, Rogers and Steinfatt, Thomas. Op. cit. pp. 223-224.
3. Hofstede, Geerte. *Cultures and Organizations Software of the Mind*. (McGraw-Hill, 1991).

Chapter 12
1. Neuliep, John and Croskey, James. "The development of a US and Generalized Ethnocentrism Scale" *Communication Research Reports*, 14 (1997): p.393.

Chapter 13
1. Beebe, B. & Redmond, M. op. cit. p. 102.
2. Ibid.
3. Levine & Adelman, op. cit. p. xix.

Chapter 14
1. Article appeared in Asahi Shinbun. Nov. 11, 2002, p. 1.
2. Ethnic Images. Chicago, National Opinion Research Center, *GSS Topical Report 10*.
3. Rogers & Steinfatt, op. cit. pp. 230-231.

Chapter 15
1. Rogers, & Steinfatt, ibid, pp. 211-215.
2. The Convention on the Elimination of All Forms of Discrimination against Women (CEDAW), adopted in 1979 by the UN General Assembly, is often described as an international bill of rights for women. It consists of a preamble and 30 articles, and defines what discrimination against women is. It set up an agenda for national action to end such discrimination.
3. Age Discrimination Employment Act effective Oct. 1, 2006 is a legal protection against age discrimination in the workplace. It is no longer lawful to discriminate on grounds of age. Treating staff fairly and recognizing individuals' talents and needs is not just the right thing to do, but makes good business sense as well.

異文化コミュニケーション関係日本語文献

八代京子他著　　『異文化トレーニング』三修社
八代京子他著　　『異文化コミュニケーション・ワークブック』三修社
西田司他著　　　『国際人間関係論』聖文社
西田ひろ子他著　『異文化間コミュニケーション入門』創元社
石井敏他著　　　『異文化コミュニケーション』有斐閣
鍋倉健悦著　　　『日本人の異文化コミュニケーション』北樹出版

本書には CD（別売）があります

Beyond Boundaries
グローバル社会の異文化コミュニケーション

2008年2月1日 初版第1刷発行
2024年2月20日 改訂新版第12刷発行

著　者　　池口　セシリア
　　　　　八代　京子

発行者　　福岡　正人
発行所　　株式会社　金星堂
　　　　（〒101-0051）東京都千代田区神田神保町 3-21
　　　　　　　　Tel.（03）3263-3828（営業部）
　　　　　　　　　　（03）3263-3997（編集部）
　　　　　　　　Fax（03）3263-0716
　　　　　　　　https://www.kinsei-do.co.jp

印刷所・製本所／株式会社カシヨ　　　Printed in Japan
本書の無断複製・複写は著作権法上での例外を除き禁じられています。本書を代行業者等の第三者に依頼してスキャンやデジタル化することは、たとえ個人や家庭内での利用であっても認められておりません。
落丁・乱丁本はお取り替えいたします。
ISBN978-4-7647-3989-5　　C1082